I0161992

ISBN 978-1-937501-03-7   1-937501-03-5

Produced by
JaDon Management Inc.
1405 4th Ave. N. W. #109
Ardmore, Ok. 73401

Original Cover Art by:
Jeffrey T. McCormack
The Pendragon Web and Graphic Design
www.thependragon.net

Jordan - V - Preston Formal Debate

James Jordan– Reformed Postmillennialist
Don K. Preston– Full (true) Preterist

+

Propositions:
Resolved: The Bible teaches that all human beings will be raised to new physical bodies at the end of the present Christian Age.

Affirm: James Jordan

Denies: Don K. Preston

Resolved: The Bible teaches that the second or final coming of Christ and the attendant resurrection from the dead, occurred at the time of the fall of Jerusalem in AD 70.

Affirm: Don K. Preston

Denies: James Jordan

Florida, 2004

Foreword by Don K. Preston

The rise in popularity of what is known as Covenant Eschatology, or full preterism– the view that all Bible prophecy was fulfilled at the end of the Old Covenant World of Israel in AD 70, has generated tremendous controversy.

Numerous written and formal public debates have been held in response to the rise of preterism. I have personally engaged in many of those debates, with representatives of the dispensational and amillennial, and postmillennial (2012) views.

In 2004 I was invited by Sam Frost of Tampa, Florida, to engage in a formal debate with James Jordan, Reformed Postmillennialist. I was tremendously honored to engage in that discussion. For years I have enjoyed and benefitted from Jordan's thoughtful and insightful writing.

Many people eschew formal debate as just "argumentation," with no good resulting. This simply is not true. When debate is conducted at a high level, with personalities set aside, and the issues themselves are the focus of the discussion much good can be, and is, accomplished. That is precisely what happened in the debate with Jordan.

Jordan was the epitome of a Christian gentleman throughout the debate, and I cannot express sufficiently my appreciation for that. I have engaged in many debates, with honorable opponents. I can honestly say that the debate with James was one of the most enjoyable debates I have ever experienced. I can also say that the feedback from the debate has likewise been overwhelmingly favorable. Those listening to the MP3s have invariably commented on the scholarly content and the cordial nature of the discussions. This is the way debate should be conducted.

It has been my longstanding desire to publish the debate in book form, and I have been encouraged repeatedly to do so. I am pleased to now offer this book in response to those requests. It is my sincere prayer that the readers of this work will find it profitable to their investigation of scripture.
Don K. Preston D. Div.
President Preterist Research Institute

Preface by James Jordan

I went into this debate with a bit of trepidation, in that I believe the "full preterist" position is a quite serious departure from the consistent teaching of every part of the Christian church for the past two millennia, and for that reason I have felt compelled over the years to say some strong things against it, though as politely as possible. My unease lay in the fact that my hosts were men who all held this position, and this might have put me in a bad position. To my relief and happiness, both Don Preston and the sponsors of this discussion were models of Christian friendliness and courtesy, who encouraged me to speak frankly. It turned out to be an enjoyable weekend.

It was pleasant to encounter Mr. Preston, who as we discovered was born on exactly the same day as myself, long ago when smilodons roamed the earth. I had read with profit his book on 2 Peter chapter 3 (*The Late Great Kingdom*) years ago, so it was nice to meet the author.

The reader will see right away that I am not a debater in the ordinary sense of the term. What I try to do in situations like this is lay out what I think are the basic Biblical presuppositions and worldview that need to inform how we approach specific passages that are at issue, and that is what I did during these discussions. It may seem as a result that Mr. Preston and I are simply talking past one another, ships passing in the night so to speak. In reality, however, the reader will find him or herself exposed quite well to the two positions, and will be in a fairly good position to compare them.

I participated in the early 1990s in an entire week of discussions and debates over this matter, with about a dozen men present. Detailed arguments took place over various passages, such as 1 Corinthians 15, at the end of which no one had budged. I frankly think that Don Preston and I made more progress in two days, and I hope that the reader of this material finds it profitable.

No changes in content have been made in my presentations. My first lecture was entirely prepared, but as is my custom, after I began to take the feel of the audience and after having heard Mr. Preston's presentation, my later talks took these into account and were perforce more informal. In line with our arrangement, I have made these informal presentations more readable by eliminating false starts, explaining hand gestures, and correcting the inevitable grammatical infelicities that occur when one is thinking on one's feet. I have not at all rewritten anything in such a way as to remove the oral nature of the presentation.

Let me end by thanking Mr. Preston for his courtesies in the past, and for making this material available.

James B. Jordan
President, Biblical Horizons Ministries

Biographical Sketch of James Jordan

James B. Jordan was born in 1949 in Athens, Georgia, into a Christian home. The descendent of a long line of Methodist, and before that Anglican ministers, Jordan's father left the increasingly liberal Methodist church around 1957 to join a conservative Lutheran church, where James was baptized and later confirmed.

Jordan attended the University of Georgia, and graduated in 1971 with an A.B. in Comparative Literature. By this time he had left Lutheranism for the Reformed (Calvinistic) understanding of the Protestant faith. He then served four years in the United States Air Force as a Military Historian, and in 1975 began attending Reformed Theological Seminary in Jackson, Mississippi. He transferred to Westminster Theological Seminary, Philadelphia, in 1979 and completed a Th.M. in Systematic Theology in 1980.

Jordan directed Geneva Ministries in Tyler, Texas, from 1980 to 1987, leaving to form Biblical Horizons, a Christian institute that he has directed ever since. (www.biblicalhorizons.com).

Jordan is author of over twenty published books, the best known of which is *Through New Eyes: Developing a Biblical View of the World.* These include full commentaries on Exodus, Judges, and Daniel.

At present Jordan is working on Zechariah. He currently serves as Dean of Biblical Studies at the Biblical Theological Seminary of St. Petersburg, Russia. In 2011 a collection of essays was presented to Jordan by his colleagues entitled *The Glory of Kings: A Festschrift in Honor of James B. Jordan.*

Biographical Sketch of Don K. Preston

Don K. Preston has been a minister since 1975. In a local capacity, he served most recently as the minister for the Ardmore church of Christ, (now known as the Ardmore Family of God) Ardmore, Ok, for 16 years.

In 2006 Preston resigned from local ministry and founded Preterist Research Institute, a non-profit organization dedicated to the teaching and defense of Covenant Eschatology, otherwise known as the full (true) preterist view of prophecy. This view- the subject of the debate in this book– says that all Bible prophecy was fulfilled at the end of the Old Covenant Age of Israel, in the destruction of Jerusalem in AD 70.

Preston is the author of 20 books on preterist (fulfilled) eschatology, including *Who Is This Babylon, The Elements Shall Melt With Fervent Heat*, and his magnum opus (to date) *We Shall Meet Him In The Air, The Wedding of the King of kings*. This book is the first and only full preterist commentary on 1 Thessalonians 4:13f ever produced, and has been widely hailed as ground-breaking.

Preston's YouTube videos, entitled "Morning Musings," are very popular. Preterist Research Institute sponsors the annual Preterist Pilgrim Weekend, a yearly seminar which is one of the most popular preterist seminars.

Preston has been described as "the leading voice of preterism today."

Preston is a popular lectureship speaker, both at home and abroad. He has engaged several leading evangelical scholars in formal public debate, as well as numerous written debates and radio debates. Some of Preston's written debates can be found on his websites: www.eschatology.org and www.bibleprophecy.com. In addition, Preston has a WordPress blog, www.donkpreston.com.

Preston is co-host, with William Bell on the popular world-wide Internet program "Two Guys and the Bible" each Tuesday night 6-7 PM (central). That program can be found at www.AD70.net.

Acknowledgements

I would be grossly remiss if I did not express my appreciation to my wife, who patiently listens as I share my research with her. She is my constant sounding board, and often asks probing questions about my thoughts that causes me to think a little more critically, a little more logically.

Debate preparation is one of the most intense kinds of research and preparation imaginable. If you have never engaged in this time consuming, intellectually challenging event, it is difficult to grasp the pressure. This often demands time not totally devoted to the wife and family. But, through it all, my wife has been, and continues to this day to be my "Rock" and constant encouragement. My appreciation for her is unbounded.

I also want to express my sincere appreciation to Natalie Murrie who volunteered to transcribe the debate. She did this because she wanted to listen to the debate as a learning experience, but, needless to say, this was a major task. She shared with me that there were some points in the tapes that were almost indecipherable.

James Jordan and I have sought to make clarifications to the MSS where listening to the tape did not settle the issue definitively. The utmost effort was made to ensure that the original thought was restored in this book. Any departure from the original thoughts is therefore, not due to any mistakes on the part of Natalie, but oversight on the part of James and myself. I am convinced that there are few – if any- such errata in the book.

Finally, my gratitude is expressed to all those who have urged me to publish this book. There were many other projects in my *que*, but, the encouragement of a host of interested parties has prompted me to finish this project. I truly hope that the finished product with bring glory to our God.

Don K. Preston's First Affirmative

As the affirmative, it is my responsibility to define my proposition.

My proposition is:
Resolved: the Bible teaches that the second, that is, the final or the eschatological coming of Christ and the attendant resurrection from the dead, occurred at the time of the fall of Jerusalem in AD 70. As in affirmative it is my responsibility to define my proposition.

Resolved: the Bible teaches all 66 books of the Bible, from Genesis to Revelation, teach us, that is, in parts, knowledge, wisdom and understanding and information, that the second, that is, the final or eschatological coming -- by that I mean that beyond the point of that coming there is not to be another resurrection like that. That this is the eschatological resurrection.

I view that as the resurrection from the dead, the death introduced by Adam in the Garden when God said, "in the day you eat, you will surely die." I believe he died that day, and I believe that the resurrection for man from that death occurred at the time of the fall of Jerusalem in AD 70. I think that's pretty much self-explanatory and it will become increasingly so hopefully, as we proceed in this discussion.

Now, I want you to take note of something. James and I agree, I believe, that the eschatological resurrection and the end of the millennium are inseparable. They are synchronous, that is to say, same time events. Therefore, if I can prove that the end of the millennium, or the resurrection, was near in the first century and was to occur at the time of the fall of Jerusalem in AD 70, I will have proven my proposition. Here then is my plan of presentation:

Number one, it is my position to show that the resurrection, the eschatological resurrection of the dead, promised in Genesis and throughout the scripture, belonged to Old Covenant Israel.

And to show from analogia scriptura, that is, analogy of scripture, that the resurrection and the end of the millennium belong to the last days of Israel.

Number four, it is my purpose to show that all of Israel's promises, therefore, inclusive of the eschatological resurrection of the dead, were fulfilled in AD 70.

And finally, to show from Revelation, if I have time to get there, that the end of the millennium was near when John wrote that book. And was, in fact, related to the time of the fall of Jerusalem in AD 70.

So point #1 in my presentation will deal with this theme, that is, the promise of the final eschatological resurrection, the end-of-the-millennium resurrection, was a promise made to Old Covenant Israel, not the church separated from, or alienated from, Israel.

Notice in Romans 8:23, Paul said that they were eagerly looking and eagerly waiting for the adoption, to wit, the redemption of the body. Now very few commentators disagree that that is resurrection, that is, the soteriological, the eschatological resurrection at the end of the millennium.

Notice that in chapter 9, Paul said, Brethren I could wish that I myself were accursed from Christ for my kinsmen, according to the flesh, those who are Israelites to whom pertain the adoption.

Now notice, that Paul said the adoption belonged to Old Covenant Israel after the flesh. But the adoption is the resurrection of the dead, Romans 8:23. Therefore, the promise of the eschatological final resurrection of the dead, to bring that resurrection life to full reality, I might say, belonged, that promise belonged, to Old Covenant Israel.

When Paul stood before Felix and Agrippa, in Acts 24, as he is accused by the Pharisees, Paul said, "They cannot prove things of which they now accuse me." They were accusing him of teaching against the Law and against the Prophets. "Nor can they prove the things of which they now accuse me. But this I confess to you, that after the way which they call a heresy, I worship the God of my Fathers, believing all things that are written in the Law and in the Prophets, ...that there is about to be [literally] the resurrection of the dead, both of the just and of the unjust."

I don't know of anyone, other than full preterists, who take that passage as predictive of anything but the final resurrection. Full preterists posit it as the final resurrection, and everyone else does, but everyone else places it still in the future.

So Acts 24 is predictive of the final resurrection. It is not one of those many resurrections typified, foreshadowed, in the Old Testament. It is in fact, the final, eschatological resurrection of the dead.

Furthermore, in Acts 26:6f, Paul said, I believe no other thing than that which is spoken by Moses and all of the Prophets, and he said, speaking to Agrippa, I stand and I'm on trial this day, believing and teaching no other things than those things written in the Law of Moses, the Psalms and the Prophets. I'm paraphrasing and conflating some verses here. But he said, "To which promise, our twelve tribes earnestly serving God day and night hope to attain..." What's the point? Paul said I'm on trial for the hope of the resurrection. That hope of the resurrection belonged to, was given to, Old Covenant Israel, the twelve tribes.

Furthermore, in 1 Corinthians 15 Paul says, "When mortal shall have put on immortality, and when corruptible shall have put on incorruptibility, then shall be brought to pass the saying, 'Death is swallowed up in victory.'" Notice he is quoting from Isaiah 25:8. Paul says the final eschatological, end-of-the-millennium resurrection which he was anticipating would be when Isaiah 25:8, and Hosea 13:14 were fulfilled.

It is absolutely critical, therefore, that we understand that the promise, the final eschatological end-of-the-millennium-resurrection-promise, belonged, and was given to, not the church separate and apart from Israel, but that promise was given to Old Covenant Israel, and simply, listen to me very carefully, reiterated, not changed -- not altered, but reiterated by the New Testament spokesmen and writers.

Now let's talk about something. James' paradigm posits, that is, his view places resurrection, that is, the end-of-the-millennium-resurrection, as *Christian eschatology*. His proposition affirms that the resurrection is yet future and will occur at the end of the current Christian age. Thus it is Christian eschatology. James says Israel's eschaton was in AD 70. However, resurrection, the final eschatological end-of-the-millennium resurrection, which Paul was anticipating in Acts 24:14-15, was the hope and the promise made to Old Covenant Israel. Now remember, it's not a type and it's not a shadow. It's not one of those many, many types of shadows of death, burial and resurrection that we see so marvelously pointed out, and that James does a great job of elucidating in his writings. This is the final resurrection, but it is a promise made to Old Covenant Israel to occur when? At the end of *her* eschaton. The end of the millennium is therefore related to the end of Israel's history.

Here is my argument, first argument really, based upon this. The law and the Prophets foretold the resurrection, that's what Paul said in Acts 24, "I believe all things that are written in the Law and the Prophets...that there is about to be the resurrection from the dead, both the just and the unjust."

Jesus, in Matthew 5, said, "Do not think that I came to destroy the Law or the Prophets. I did not come to destroy, but to fulfill. For verily I say unto you, until heaven and earth passes away, not one jot nor one tittle shall pass from the law until it is *all* fulfilled."

Now follow the argument, please. The Law and the Prophets foretold the resurrection, now that includes the Law. Jesus said, not one iota of the Law, which predicted the resurrection, could pass until the totality, not part of it, not some of it, not even most of it, but *none* of it could pass until the totality of it was fulfilled.

Therefore, since the resurrection was part of the Law , and since *all* of the Law had to be fulfilled before *any* of the Law could pass, it follows that if the resurrection, the eschatological final end-of-the-millennium resurrection, has not occurred, then the totality of the old law, which includes animal sacrifices, remains valid and binding today.

Jesus did not say the Old Covenant will be transformed and then at the end of that transformed Old Covenant, everything will pass. He said until that old law, the Mosaic Covenant, the Mosaic Torah, until that's fulfilled, *none* of it will pass away.

All right, the question is, well, does James believe that all of the old law remains valid and binding today? No, I asked him a written question, and one of the questions was, "In what mode of time and with what event were all of God's promises made to Old Covenant Israel fulfilled and his covenant relationship with them terminated?" And he said well that was in AD 70.

Furthermore, in a series of tapes reviewing Max King and his teachings, James said, "AD 70 was the end, not just of the Mosaic world, but of the entire Adamic world of Genesis 2 -3."

Now I would make the following argument, that the Adamic world of Genesis 2-3, is the world of sin and death. If, therefore, the entire Adamic world of Genesis 2 through 3 was removed in AD 70, I would insist that the resurrection, the eschatological resurrection, has occurred.

All right, here's the argument again. Notice that Jesus said *none* of the old law, *not one iota* of it could pass until it was all fulfilled. All of that old law was fulfilled by AD 70, according to James. Therefore, the resurrection had to have occurred in AD 70.

Here's the quote again: AD 70 was the end, not just of the Mosaic world, but of the entire Adamic world of Genesis 2-3. But all of the Mosaic law, including resurrection, that's what Paul says in Acts 24, had to be fulfilled before that Old Covenant world could pass away, Matthew 5: 17-18. Therefore, if the Mosaic world has passed, as James says it has, then the resurrection must have occurred.

I want to take a look at a couple of passages here, both of which I understand – if I'm wrong here, James can correct me, but in our conversations this is what I've gleaned, and from his writings and from his tapes, I've gleaned this – he believes that Daniel 12 and Matthew 13 both speak of the same time and event.

Daniel 12 foretold the time of the end, the end of the age, if you please, and the time of the resurrection "of those who sleep in the dust of the earth shall arise some to everlasting life some to everlasting damnation." And that would occur when the "righteous would shine forth as the sun." Well, Jesus in Matthew 13 said that the harvest at the end of the age when the son of man would come and gather together the righteous, gather together the elect, would be when Daniel 12:3 would be fulfilled.

Now again James agrees with me that both of these refer to the end of the age in AD 70. When would that be fulfilled? Daniel 12:7 is explicit. When the power of the holy people has been completely shattered, all of these things shall be fulfilled. There is thus unequivocal evidence right here that the end of the age, the harvest resurrection, is associated with the end of Israel's age.
The great question is, do Daniel 12 and Matthew 13 deal with the same harvest and the same resurrection as the other eschatological passages that we find in the New Testament?

Well, let us notice something. Paul says in 1 Corinthians 15:19 that Christ was the first fruits of the harvest. I think we have a perfectly legitimate right to ask, will the harvest, and/or upon what basis would we delineate from the harvest of 1 Corinthians 15 which would happen at the time of the end at the coming of the Lord from the harvest at the time of the end at the coming of the Lord in Matthew 13 – when both of these passages are dealing with the fulfillment of promises, Old Covenant promises, made to Israel?

Now let me go ahead with this. Christ was the first fruit of the harvest, 1 Corinthians 15:19f. Now I want you to notice something very carefully. Christ's resurrection was in the end "of the age." At the end of what age was Jesus resurrected as the first fruit? Well, very clearly it wasn't at the end of the Christian age, was it? He appeared at the end of the age to put away sin by the sacrifice of himself. He was resurrected in that same end of the age.

Now watch this. In Matthew 13:39-40 Jesus said the harvest of which he would be the first fruit would be at "the end of this age." Now here's the question–first of all, a point. Harvest and first fruit are in the analogy of scripture, and in scripture, harvest and first fruit belong to the same season. You don't gather the first fruit in one season and the harvest 20 years later. They belong to the same season. To posit the harvest at the end of the Christian age, the harvest of which Jesus was first fruit, and he was raised as the first fruit at the end of the Old Covenant age, to posit the harvest at the end of the Christian age removes it, that is the resurrection, from the time of the first fruit and places the harvest in a totally different season. And I would say that is untenable and a violation of scripture.

Now, James and I certainly agree that the resurrection of 1 Corinthians 15 is the resurrection of Revelation 20, the end-of-the-millennium resurrection. If, therefore, I can show that the resurrection of 1 Corinthians 15 was in AD 70, I will have proven my proposition and have proven that the millennium ended in AD 70.

Let's take a look. At the close of Paul's extended discussion of resurrection in 1 Corinthians 15, he focuses on three issues:

Number one, he says that this resurrection which he was anticipating and foretelling would be the fulfillment of Israel's promises. He quotes from Isaiah 25 and Hosea 13.

Secondly, this time of the resurrection would be the time of the removal of the Law that was the strength of sin, verse 56.

Point number 3, he says that this resurrection would be the time of the removal of the sting of death, that is, sin, verse 56. Let's proceed to take a look at each of these three elements that are so central and vital to Paul's discussion of resurrection.

I want to call your attention to Daniel 9. Daniel was told 70 weeks are determined on your people and upon your holy city. Unequivocally this is not a prediction of the end of the Christian age. This has to do with Old Covenant Israel and her history.

Now watch this. It is not therefore about the church, nor is it a prediction of the end of the church age. I must make this observation: the Bible is unequivocal that the current kingdom in which we live is without end. How can we even discuss the end of the current Christian age when the Bible, speaking of the Christian age says, "Unto Him that is, God, be glory in the church by Jesus Christ throughout all generations, age without end. Hebrews 12 says the kingdom they were then receiving, that was shortly to be consummated, would never be removed.

In contrast to the Old Covenant kingdom that went through eschatological transformation, the writer of Hebrews says the kingdom they were then receiving would never be removed; it would never go through eschatological transformation to put an end to it. I think that is extremely, extremely critical.

All right, notice that Daniel was told 70 weeks are determined to seal, most translations say "seal up;" it's "seal," vision and prophecy. To seal vision and prophecy means confirmation through fulfillment. In my book, SEAL UP VISION AND PROPHECY, on the table back there, there is 99.9 per cent agreement in the scholarly world that that's exactly what it means.

I want you to notice that it does not say, "seal A vision and prophecy." Nor does it say, "seal THE vision and prophecy." The definite article is not in the Hebrew. And most commentators regardless of their eschatological paradigm, most scholars that I have consulted on Daniel 9 agree, one shape, form or other, the interpretation they differ on, but they nonetheless agree that Daniel was being told that by the end of the 70 weeks all prophecy, all vision would be sealed up through fulfillment.

In other words, Daniel 9 foretold the time of the fulfillment of *all* prophecy – not *some* of it, not *a little bit* of it, not even *most* of it – but a vision and prophecy comprehensively considered. All right, I want you to notice, please.
All prophecy would be fulfilled by the end of the 70 weeks of Daniel 9.
But the end of the 70 weeks of Daniel 9 would be AD 70 because the end of that vision is the desolation of the city (v 27) to the end. The end of what? Seventy weeks. That's the antecedent. To the end desolations are determined. It shall come in "like a flood." The end of the 70 weeks of Daniel 9 would be AD 70.
Therefore all prophecy would be fulfilled by AD 70.

Now that agrees perfectly with what Jesus said as he foretold of the destruction of Jerusalem of AD 70 when he said in Luke 21:22 describing that event, "These be the days of vengeance In which all things that are written must be fulfilled."

Now watch this. All promises to Israel – let's just focus on the promises to Israel, all right – would be fulfilled by the end of the 70 weeks of Daniel – AD 70. But the promise of the resurrection of 1 Corinthians 15, the end-of-the-millennium resurrection of Revelation 20, was a promise made to Old Covenant Israel (Isaiah 25, Hosea 13). Therefore, the promise of the resurrection was fulfilled by the end of the 70 weeks, that is AD 70.

Now watch this, the promise of the resurrection, being a promise made to Old Covenant Israel, belonging to Israel after the flesh – that doesn't mean it would be a fleshly physical resurrection, but that promise was given to her and belonged to her – the promise of the resurrection being a promise to Israel was fulfilled by the end of the 70 weeks. But the resurrection is posited at the end of the millennium. Therefore, the end of the millennium was fulfilled by the end of the 70 weeks, in other words by AD 70.

Now let's look a little bit closer at Paul's focus in 1 Corinthians 15. Paul said that the resurrection would be when the Law, that is the strength of sin, was removed. The question is, what law was the strength of sin? Well, I asked James that question in my written questions to him. Here is his response:

"My first order reading would be that THE sin," notice that, I like that, "THE sin is the impurities of the levitical system and death [and I would add THE death] is uncleanness. This type of logical, though real form of law, sin and death, has passed away, but behind it is Genesis 2 thru 3."

Now I want you notice carefully what this means. "The Law, that is the strength of sin, is Genesis 2 through 3." That's his answer to my question number 10. However, in his tapes he said AD 70 was the end, not just of the Mosaic world, *but of the entire Adamic world of Genesis 2 through 3.* Now, if Genesis 2 through 3 lies behind 1 Corinthians 15, as the Law that was the strength of sin, and if the entire Adamic world of Genesis 2 through 3 was removed and replaced in AD 70, then the resurrection occurred in AD 70.

Let's go on. The Law, when we see that term, "the Law," in Paul -- it is used 117 times. It is used without a modifier 110 times. In other words, Paul simply says the Law, the Torah. Only 17 times is it used with modifiers, and those modifiers help us determine that it is *not* the Mosaic law -- "the law of the spirit of life in Christ Jesus" (Romans 8). Invariably, when the term, "the Law," is used without a qualifier, it is the Mosaic Law.

Paul said, "I was alive without the Law. The commandment came, sin revived, and I died." What was he talking about? Well, it's pretty clear: "I'd not known sin except the Law said, 'Thou shalt not covet.'" I know what law that is – Mosaic Law. 2 Corinthians 3, he spoke of "The Law, that is, the ministration of death." In Galatians 3, he says, "those who are under the Law are under the curse." Very clearly, that's not the gospel, unless we're under a curse under the gospel of Christ.

All right, let's go on just a little bit.

The resurrection would be when the Law that was the strength of sin would be removed.

But the Law in Paul's writings is the Mosaic Law, and James says that's the first reading of it.

Therefore the resurrection would be when the Mosaic Law would be removed.

All right, let's look at point number three of Paul's focus in 1 Corinthians 15. I want you to notice: Daniel was told seventy weeks are determined to put away sin. The time of the putting away of sin is the time of the resurrection (1 Corinthians 15). [I'm going to have to speed up here because I've already been given a cue, and I can't believe that. I really tried to slow down for you.] Anyway, the time of the putting away of the sin is the time of the resurrection, unequivocally. Therefore, the resurrection at the end of the millennium would be at the end of the 70 weeks, that is in AD 70.

I want you to catch the power now of the comparison of Daniel 9 and 1 Corinthians 15. Both deal with promises made to Israel. Both deal with the time of the end. Both deal with the time of the kingdom. Both deal with the time of the putting away of sin, and both deal with the end of Israel's age. Daniel 9:27, the full end. 1 Corinthians 15, resurrection. When? When the law that was the strength of sin would be removed. Thus, both passages deal with Israel and her history.

Now watch this. Here's the argument.

Daniel 9 and 1 Corinthians 15 foretold the same event – the putting away of sin, resurrection.

1 Corinthians 15 would be fulfilled at the end of the millennium. However, Daniel 9 which is the parallel to 1 Corinthians 15 would be fulfilled in AD 70.

Therefore, the end of the millennium would be in AD 70.

Now I want you to notice something. The final end of the millennium, the resurrection, was the hope of Israel. Paul says this over and over again. But all of God's promises to Old Covenant Israel were fulfilled by AD 70. I asked James that question, at what point of time, and with what event were all of God's promises to Old Covenant Israel fulfilled, and his covenant relationship with them terminated. He said, "AD 70."

All right:

The final, end of the millennium resurrection was the hope of Israel.

But, all of God's promises to Israel were fulfilled by AD 70.

Therefore, the final end-of-the-millennium resurrection being the hope of Israel was fulfilled in AD 70.

Let me summarize. What have we seen so far? We have seen that resurrection at the end of the millennium belongs to Old Covenant Israel and belongs to her last days. Resurrection is not Christian eschatology. Jesus, as Scott McKnight says, never looked beyond AD 70 in his eschatology, and I suggest to you neither did Paul or Peter. They only looked to the end of the fulfillment of God's promises to Israel. Thus, resurrection at the end of the millennium belongs to Israel and thus her last days.

Secondly, Israel's promises had to be fulfilled before the law could pass, and we have seen that all of Israel's promises were fulfilled by AD 70.

We have shown that the end of the millennium, the time of the harvest of Matthew 13 was fulfilled in AD 70. We have seen that the end of the millennium promise of the resurrection of 1 Corinthians 15 belonged to Israel's last days when the old law which was the strength of sin was removed and that would be at the end of the 70 weeks in Daniel 9.

Here then is our conclusion. We have proven that the text that James applied, 1 Corinthians 15, to the end of the Christian age belonged to AD 70, the end of Old Covenant Israel's aeon. We have shown secondly, that the end of the millennium resurrection text belonged to AD 70. It seems to me, therefore, that we have proven our proposition.

Let me say again. Neither Jesus, nor Paul, nor Peter, ever looked beyond the promises made to Israel for their resurrection hope. We sometimes say, as is common, resurrection is at the end of **this** age. Jesus, living in the Old Covenant age, said harvest is at the end of **this** age. He was the first fruit of that resurrection which was through the current the end of **that** age, not at the end of the Christian age, which has no end. Okay, thank you very much.

James Jordan's First Negative

I have never done one these kinds of things before so I really didn't know what to expect or how to prepare. So, since we were told this morning that it was just going to be ships passing in the dark anyway, there's not going to be any interaction between the two of us (*wink*), I'm just going to mosey on with what I have.

Just a couple of comments which you might be able to say something about, Don -- and this is not any type of refutation -- but in Daniel 12, I read in verse two that "many of those who sleep in the dust of the ground will awake, these to everlasting life and others to disgrace and contempt." That "many" is, I think, a difficulty for any expositor, whether he's a traditional futurist who puts this at the end of time, or someone linking it with the AD 70 event. It's for that reason I think that what this refers to here is Jesus' work in his earthly life. That he went through Israel cleansing lepers, cleansing those who had issues of blood (and "cleansing" means resurrection), actually raising a few people from the dead and in general restoring Israel to life one last time before they fell again and rejected God again by putting Jesus to death.

Pretty much all the miracles Jesus does have to do with the Levitical requirements, so my own inclination on this verse is to link it with what Jesus himself does since it's not "all," it's "many." Some are raised to life, others defile that life and of course, in this same time there's a tribulation and the righteous shine like stars, and Paul makes that allusion, as well.

One other thought I'll be coming back to, if time permits, that the law brings death in 1 Corinthians 15 and obviously other places. Absolutely. So did the violation of law concerning the tree of the knowledge of good and evil. My understanding of the death aspect of the Torah is that it is the republication and amplification of that original disobeying of the law. Part of my observation here is that the deaths that are associated with the Mosaic system have this symbolic character. They involve being estranged from the worship of the tabernacle as a result and it's entirely fitting that a resurrection come for Israel that removes *that* kind of estrangement. In Adam's case that estrangement is there but so is eventual physical death, and that implies to me that there is a larger history of the world within which the history of Israel is a typological aspect, and I will be coming to that in some detail. But I think once I have digested what I just heard, perhaps I can interact with it a little bit more concretely.

So let me in the next 20 minutes or so, just move into what I prepared to do. Our two topics are very similar and I think we'll both be giving arguments that maybe by the end we'll be able to talk to each other more fully. I want to lay a few more things out, and that is, the importance of the physical sign of life in biblical religion. I think there are some pre-suppositional matters here that are, at the best, fuzzy.

Max King's first book has got some really radically gnostic elements to it when he talks about physical versus spiritual, and he corrects that in his second book, in the great big, huge, fat book, and seeks to avoid the dangers in what certainly looks like Greek influence of his thinking. This is a tricky matter because the Bible uses words like body, flesh, and spirit and it's not always clear exactly what it means -- it's not always clear that the connotations are the same in every passage.

Paul says flesh and blood are not going to inherit the kingdom of God, 1 Corinthians 15. Well, okay, but, of course, flesh and blood do inherit the kingdom of God. Every Lord's Day you have the flesh and blood of Jesus Christ, so in some sense flesh and blood have inherited the kingdom of God and is given to you to give you new flesh and new blood. It's going to have to depend on what the context indicates with phrases like that. So, I think it's good to at least reflect on this matter.

Now, the New Testament is simply the continuation of the completion of the scriptures and we've got one Bible here. We need to think about the tradition of writing and understanding in Israel. That is to say, that you have a school of people, priests and Levites, who have the major understanding and conception of what's been said already – who've meditated on it a whole lot and who are the people that God can use to add to it when a new book is needed, when a new phase of revelation has come about. And this is written in scribal Hebrew. This Hebrew that the Bible is written in is not conversational Hebrew.

Studies have been made on this. This is a written language, a scribal language – doesn't change very much over a thousand years. There're not enough grammatical forms for this to be an actual spoken language. It's a scribal language. You have that today even in French language. You have a past tense, a "passe simple," which is never used in spoken French; it only occurs in written French. In all the ancient world there were these priestly scribal versions of the language – some were more technical. Words were used over and over again so as to build up certain concepts and associations. And the New Testament is within this. The New Testament books are all to the Jew first, to those who lived within this tradition, and who were therefore the best able to understand the allusions and quotations that are found in every paragraph of what we call the New Testament.

It's quite different from the Old – very seldom you find in a prophetic book a quotation from something earlier. There are plenty of allusions, not very many quotations, but in the New Testament it's hard to find a paragraph where there's not something that's quoted from the Old. It's as if really the New Testament is just a commentary on the Old Testament. It's just a footnote to the Old. The Old Testament is the real Bible, he said – being an Old Testament-type guy. (*wink*)

Well, all of which is to say the New Testament writings assume a radical and thorough familiarity with the Old. Not merely a familiarity with random details, but a familiarity with the world view pre-suppositions and philosophy of history that is taught throughout the warp and woof of the Old. I'm sure we all agree on this. The prophecies found in the New Testament writings are not intended to stand on their own to be interpreted merely by comparing them with each other. They have to be understood in terms of foundation, a world view, a philosophy of reality and history that have been laid down repeatedly in multiple ways over a very long period of time. The New Testament was written to people shaped by this tradition, which was quite different from the traditions of other peoples. The scriptures shaped these people to understand an absolute distinction between the creator and the creature, so that no man and nothing within the universe partook of divinity in even the most infinitesimal degree.

Hence, right away the church understood that though Jesus is both God and man there is no mixture of the two. There is no uncreated divinity in his humanity and no created humanity in his divinity. There is one person, two natures. The scriptures had also shaped the Jews to understand and believe in the goodness of the creation. From the beginning, both the creation and human beings were places where the Spirit dwelled.

Let me just remind you of what it actually says in Genesis 1. "In the beginning, God created the heavens and the earth. The earth was shapeless, and empty, and darkness was over the surface of the deep, and the Spirit of God was moving over the surface of the water." See, it doesn't actually say God sent the Spirit into the world. He's there. He's not part of the world. But the act of creating the world *is* the act of sending the Spirit into it. The Spirit travels with the world bringing it from glory to glory and that starts right here. Then when man is made, "Then Yahweh God formed man from the dust of the ground and breathed into his nostrils breath of life," -- spirit of life. It's the same word in Hebrew - *ru'ahh* - "and man became a living soul," whatever that word soul means – okay? That's one of those tricky things.

Right from the beginning human beings are houses of the Holy Spirit. You can't be alive without it. There is a first form of spirituality that is thoroughly physical. Both in the world which is the house in which the Spirit is moving, and moving from glory to glory, and in this physical body which the Spirit is going to be working with. The scriptures that shaped the Jews to understand that the future of the world did not in any way think it meant leaving behind the physicality of it. We just know this from all the writings of the Jews in Jesus' day. They did not believe in some kind of a movement into a higher or different plane of existence. But rather the future means a transfiguration of the physical universe and human body to a glorified physicality in which the Spirit would dwell more fully than He originally dwelt.

Now, in Acts 17 the apostle Paul encountered Greek philosophers who thought in quite a different way. For them, the world would go on forever, returning in endless cycles. There would be no judgment, no transfiguration of the cosmos into a new and permanent glorious condition. For them the world of matter and physicality was inferior to a higher world, if not downright evil. After death, men existed as souls without bodies permanently in conditions ranging from misery to happiness. Some few men might be deified upon death and become gods moving high up the scale of being, but they were few in number and always persons who had been mighty and powerful in this life.

Now, I want to give my view on a couple of verses in Acts 17. Verse 18 tells us who these guys were. "Also some of the Epicurean and Stoic philosophers were disputing with Paul. Some were saying, 'What would this idle babbler wish to say?' Others, 'He seems to be a proclaimer of strange demons,' because he was preaching Jesus and the resurrection. And so they took him and brought him to the Areopagus, the hill of Mars, saying, 'May we know what this new teaching is that you are proclaiming, for you are bringing some strange things to our ears, and we want to know what these things mean.' Now all the Athenians and strangers visiting there used to spend their time in nothing other than telling or hearing something new." Now this is one of the real funny passages in the Bible, of course, because Paul tells them the one thing that is really new and they can't stand it. So, so much for wanting to hear new things!

Well, the Stoics and the Epicureans both despised the physical body. For the Stoics the body was a problem to be fought by avoiding passionate emotion. This idea has influenced the church a whole lot, historically. You'll see an example of it in a minute. For the Epicureans, the body was irrelevant. If it wants to run wild, let it, so what? All that matters is the mind and the spirit. All this is quite different from the Old Testament picture. The body is very important and engages fully in the worship of God through exuberant praise with cymbals and trumpets and dance. What is more emotional than the cries, the screams of the psalmists when they are suffering and they cry out to God? The body is neither suppressed nor ignored, but rather is precisely the means by which God is worshiped, not least of all by eating at feasts and festivals.

Now go back to Acts 17, verses 30-32. I want to really focus on a detail here. Paul ends his message, which we don't have time to look at in detail, and we don't need to. He says, "Therefore, having overlooked the times of ignorance, God is now declaring to men that all everywhere should repent because he has fixed a day in which he will judge the *oikoumene*...." This means the Roman empire at that point in time. It means this thing that God set up in the book of Daniel – it went through Babylon, Persia, the four Greek phases, and then the final Roman imperial phase, and then it's going to come to an end. The New Testament is not just concerned about the end of Israel, it's also concerned about the end of this *oikoumene*, the land around the land. And Acts begins to move into that. In the book of Acts is the penetration of that word of coming judgment into the Greeks as well. Watch in the New Testament when it says Greek and when it says Gentile. Those don't mean the same thing. Greek means inhabitant of the *oikoumene*, this person who's in God's bigger land, the land around the land, the new land that comes after the exile.

I might as well say this, too: You know, the promises that God made to Abraham really in an important way were over when they went back to Babylon. When you're at Ur of the Chaldees, you have the Tower of Babel, the division of the humanity into many religions and then many languages connected with that. Then you come out of Ur of the Chaldees into the land, the land of promise. It's a crummy, third rate land, full of famine, doesn't feed you -- some type of huge problem with this land. Then we go down to Egypt and we come back, and hey, the land has become a land that flows with milk and honey. The land is resurrected. And we live there for a while and then we go back to Babylon. And then there's another Tower of Babel in the book of Daniel, isn't there, in chapter 5. They're confused at what they read on the wall instead of confused by what they hear. It's the same judgment, judgment of the second Babylon.

When does the judgment on the third Babylon start? When is the third confusion of tongues? It's Acts 2, isn't it? You see, God confuses Babylons. So we've come back. You know, we say, well, the Jews returned from exile. Well, not really -- they didn't go back to the same land they had before. It's much smaller, but it's now holy land. Never called the holy land before – after the exile, it's the holy land. And that means that the Jews have been relieved of the burden of having their own king and army. They don't have to worry about that stuff anymore. They can devote themselves to religious work exclusively. They're in this much smaller land, but the whole land is holy. Jerusalem is there, and it's called a holy city – never a holy city before

– the city of David; now it's the holy city. There is a land, but the land is this empire that surrounds them. There is a real change in configuration that happens here and that is the beginning, the first phase, the anticipatory phase of the New Covenant. It really starts there.

So the New Testament is concerned with the end of Israel, but it's also concerned with end of this *oikoumene*. Both of them are going to be judged in the 60s. Old Rome will be burned down, the imperial line will be completely destroyed. There'll be chaos. The same kinds of things are happening in Israel. I believe you have to keep an eye on both of those things. And here is Paul – watch what happens here. Verse 30-32. He says, "He has fixed a day (verse 31) in which he will judge this *oikoumene* in righteousness through a man whom he has appointed, having furnished proof to all men by raising him from the dead."

Now, for these philosophers, the notion of a coming judgment on the *oikoumene* is not a scandal. But I didn't yet read verse 32, did I? "When they heard of the resurrection of the dead, some began to sneer. Others said, 'We will hear you again concerning this.'" The notion of a coming judgment on the *oikoumene* is not a scandal. In this cyclical world empires rise and empires fall but philosophy goes on and on. That's not a problem. What scandalized them was what Paul said about the resurrection of Jesus. Well, what did he say? Well we don't really know in detail, do we? This is just a condensed version of what he talked to them about all afternoon long on the Areopagus.

But if Paul had proclaimed that Jesus had died and appeared in some kind of spirit form and ascended into heaven, this would not have scandalized them. That would have just been one more story of a divinized hero. No, the thing that would cause them to scoff would be the notion of a physical resurrection, an affirmation of the goodness, and I submit, eventual glorification of the physical body of human beings. They don't sneer at the notion of judgment because their thinking can absorb that. They sneer at the notion of a carnal, earthly and material eschatology, for such an idea, for them, is gross and ridiculous.

And just to follow-up on what I was saying a moment ago, this judgment of the *oikoumene*, verse 33, is very important. The very next thing we read, "So Paul went out of their midst." That's an obvious allusion back to Matthew 23 and 24 when Jesus walks out of Jerusalem, and that's it. Jerusalem was now toast. They'll be given one more chance and then that's it. Just as Ezekiel saw the Lord move out of the city and the great vision of the abominations of desolation, Ezekiel 8-10. Well, here Paul walks out and as the Jews rejected Jesus, so the *oikoumene* rejected Paul and judgment is going to be the result.

Well, now here in this passage, I submit, we see a clear contrast between biblical and the most sophisticated of pagan world views. This contrast can be seen in worship. For the pagan worship is a way of getting out of the body. And hence even the most physical aspects of pagan worship, such as furious dancing and sexual intercourse with priests and priestesses, are ways of cultivating mystical out-of-body experiences, ecstatic experiences, which are, of course, necessarily private and individual. That's what mystical experience is. That's always something *you* get. Who knows what the person next to you is doing. You don't wind up dreaming the same dream as other people at the same time. I've never heard of that: Eight people all having a mystical experience and all seeing each other together in it? It doesn't work that way. It's totally private.

For God's people worship is by means of the physical body. It involves bodily people acting together in singing, dancing, hand clapping, hand raising. It involves people together playing loud musical instruments, trumpets, cymbals, and mass strings. It involves eating together at feasts and festivals. Nowhere in the Psalms is worship ever pictured as getting out of the body, as any kind of private mystical experience. Prophetic visions may be like that, but not worship. Worship is by means of the body. The body is necessary for the fullness of the worship of God. And so David asks, "Can the grave praise you?" How can the dead praise since they have no voices, they have no bodies? It doesn't work.

This is my argument. The Jews had worshiped this way for a thousand years by Jesus' time. Worship in the old tabernacle was silent. When the king comes, you take up instruments and sing in the new temple.

That's what the fourth book of the Psalms says. The fourth book is a narrative that describes the coming of the king and what happens when the king comes. When the king comes, you take up instruments and sing. Before that time, you just talked. You see the same thing in Revelation 4 and 5. When the king goes to heaven, the angels stop talking; they pick up instruments and start singing.

The Jews had been worshiping this way for a thousand years. It would never have occurred to them, I submit, that the worship offered by the dead without physical bodies who can't, aren't holding on to harps and things any more -- it would never have occurred to them that worship offered by disembodied souls would be higher and better than in-body worship.

Now for the pagan, it's exactly the opposite. The body is the tomb, *soma sema* – the body is the tomb. And worship means contemplation or some other kind of mystical way of getting out of the body. The dead are better able to praise God since they don't have this bodily hindrance holding them down. Now, I think all this would be clearer to us if our own protestant tradition of worship wasn't so pagan. Where are our cymbals and trumpets? Where do we clap hands? Where are the shouts of praise? Well, not with us! Well, maybe with some of you, since times are beginning to change. But, at least in Reformed circles, and in the more intellectual Christian circles that are very teaching-centered, it's all brain to brain communication. It's as disembodied as possible.

Paul says, "Be filled with the spirit, singing songs and playing instruments." When he says, "singing psalms and making music," that "make music" is a quotation from Psalm 98. Singing and playing instruments is what it is about. There's no a capella singing anywhere in the Bible. Note how often the church has thought a capella singing was better, and also slow singing. In the Bible, worship singing always involves the use of the physical creation to make accompanying loud music.

And how do we eat and worship? We sit around and look at each other at the table? No, we crouch over ourselves and seek a private moment with God. There's not enough bread to chew and not enough wine to get any effect. If you even use wine. The Corinthians had a problem with some people getting drunk at the supper. Folks, if we were biblical in our worship, that would be our problem. We don't have that problem. We're not like the apostolic church. It'd be better if we had that problem. Instead, we've minimized every physical aspect of things.

Our worship betrays us. Worshiping as we do is not surprising – most Christians think more about going to heaven when they die, than about getting new physical bodies to praise God with in the fullness of time. Your average Joe Christian out there hasn't really thought about what the Nicene Creed says about the bodily resurrection. If you ask him point blank, he says, "Oh, yeah, I believe in the resurrection," but really all of his hymns and all of his piety is connected with becoming disembodied. I submit to you that an ancient Jew just would not have recognized that.

The contrast between biblical and pagan world views can also be see in the nature of salvation. Both agree that humanity is estranged from nature. For the pagan, that's just how it is. And salvation means getting out of nature, getting away from it. "This world is not my home." Some day I'll get out of it. The biblical understanding is that the estrangement of humanity from nature is a result of the fall. Nature is on God's side, and thus is against us.

When Adam fell, the roses came to God and said, "We would like to grow thorns to teach this sinner a lesson. We don't want him putting his filthy sinful hands on us. May we grow some thorns?" And God said, "Sure." Then the tiger said, "We'd like to take a bite out of crime; is that okay?" And God said, "Yeah." The world is against us because the world is on God's side. The world is not cursed. We must read Genesis 3:17. It says, "Cursed is the ground with reference to you." God's judgment will be mediated to us through the creation. Creation is on God's side. They like to see us suffer, because we deserve to suffer. That's their attitude.

Well, I'm being slightly facetious, but that's the picture. From the biblical point of view, salvation means that when men are made right, they are in harmony with nature. Wild animals are no longer against men. They become tame as Isaiah's vision shows. However you take that vision, it is a vision of nature and men restored. Probably has more to do with other nations – what it's talking about indirectly. But the imagery used, you see, is a restored man-and-nature link. Unproductive lands happily tossing up famines against Canaanites will become lands that flow with milk and honey. This is the meaning of the vision in Genesis 15. The two sides of the divided animals represent Abram and the land. They are both dead to each other. But God's spirit passes between them which means they are knit together, reunited into a resurrected existence, glorified, and that will come in 400 years. Abraham will be glorified into a people and the land will go from being "famine city" to being a land that flows with milk and honey. Just look at it: Abraham and Lot could not live in the same area. The land was so unproductive. Look at all the people who were able to live together 400 years later.

The various ecological laws, such as the law against cutting down fruit trees, the law against taking both baby and mother birds, the law of Sabbath years, all are pointing to the fact that restoration and resurrection of men is to bring with it restoration and resurrection of the natural physical world. Far from leaving this world, restored man brings the world with him to God, both in his care for it and when he brings it in the grain and wine of the Tribute offering. Formed by this thinking for nearly 2,000 years, is the Jew now suddenly to believe that salvation, resurrection, glorification means leaving this world behind? Well, I just don't think so.

So far from believing this, the Christian teaching has always been that the physical world is transformed right along with the physical bodies and human beings at the end. In fact, in most of the tradition of the church is also the belief that animals will also be resurrected along with human beings because animals are semi-persons, as all of you know who have dogs or cats. Why should they be left behind? After all, Noah brought the animals with him from the old to the new world.

In summary, the Bible consistently teaches against paganism, orating on intense physicality. The creation is good and necessary for the fullness of worship and praise by human beings. In the physical cosmos it's tied to humanity and travels with it. I submit that once your thinking is formed by this, it becomes unthinkable that full salvation means leaving this physicality behind. So that's what we have to say on that subject, as Calvin would say, and our two presentations are starting light years apart, but maybe we'll move together and be able to interact at some point.

Don K. Preston's Second Affirmative

Let me say at the outset of my second presentation here that I'll not be responding here to anything that James said. I'm saving my third spot – my third affirmative – to try to respond to some of the things that he had to say because I do want to address a few of the issues that he raised but for the time being in my second affirmative I want to lay out some more material. And by the way, let me say this: I know that I'm going to present far more material than James could ever get to in rebuttal and I don't expect him to get every single point, but I certainly would advise him to take some of the points and discuss them and give his side of the story as it were.

Let me continue with my presentation that has to do with that the resurrection, the end of the millennium resurrection, regardless of what we conceive it to be, all right – because you see it really doesn't matter what our concept is at this juncture. We have to bring it in harmony and in line and in unity with when the Bible says it would occur and the framework in which that resurrection, the end of the millennium resurrection would occur.

Now I'm going to present a series of arguments. They're going to be wide-ranging, all right, but the purpose of these arguments is to demonstrate, like my first one, that the end of the end of the millennium resurrection really was near in the first century. I'm going to begin by trying to demonstrate to you that the resurrection began in Jesus' personal ministry and consummated in AD 70.

I think it's kind of interesting that James in some of his tapes said that 30 to 70 was "a kind of millennium." But then he believes that the millennium of Revelation 20 began in AD 70, not in the personal ministry. Well I want you to notice the absolute parallels between Jesus' ministry, the life of the early church and Revelation 20.

In Jesus' ministry he sent his disciples out on what we sometimes call one of the limited commissions, and they came back rejoicing that the demons were subject to them. And Jesus' response was, "I saw Satan cast from heaven." Well, what does Revelation 20 show us. "I saw an angel in great chains come out of heaven and he bound Satan and cast him down into the bottomless pit."

In Ephesians 2:5f, Paul is speaking to those whom he said had been dead and raised to life to sit in the heavenly places on thrones. They're now on thrones just like those in Revelation chapter 20 are on thrones. Also, in Revelation 20:6, those on the thrones are priests. Just like John said, Revelation 1:5, speaking to living breathing human beings at the time, he has made us to be a kingdom, and that's what Revelation 20 is all about, isn't it? The millennium kingdom. "He has made us to be a kingdom of kings and priests." And then, of course, Jesus predicted the coming resurrection, there was an already, but the not-yet resurrection. John 5, just as in Revelation 20 there is an already, but a not-yet. There is, therefore, a perfect correlation between these two concepts and these two time periods.

By the way, I developed an awful lot of this material, not all of it, some of this is brand new in my personal studies, at least, but most of this material is in my book, WHO IS THIS BABYLON, so you can help yourself.

Now I want to go back to Matthew 13 and deal with this passage, even though James does believe now, he didn't when I – I listened to some tapes, and in the tape that I was listening to, James said Matthew 13:39f is very clearly the end of the current Christian age. Last night I asked him if he still believed that, and he said, "I don't think I do."

Well, I have to tell you I appreciate that mentality. I'm willing to change. I'd be glad to go back to the a-millennial world. I'd be glad to go post millennial, if somebody can convince me. But I do appreciate that attitude very much. But I want to use Matthew 13 to show you something.

Matthew 13:39f is the end of the millennium resurrection, I believe, because it's the resurrection at the end of the age at the coming of the Lord, and again, James used to believe that. But Matthew 13:39f was fulfilled in AD 70 as we both now agree. Therefore, if it is, in fact, the end of the millennium resurrection of Revelation 20 it was fulfilled in AD 70. Let's go on just a little bit more. The resurrection at the end of the millennium, I cannot drive this home enough – James brought up Acts 17, and he spoke about, "Well that was the coming judgment on the *oikoumene*."

Well, here's the point – the judgment of Acts 17 is the end of the millennium judgment. And Paul said it was "about to" take place. I don't care if you make it the Roman world. I don't care if you make it – America, you know – it's related to the end of the millennium resurrection of which Paul is discussing and Paul said it was about to take place. And that resurrection of Acts 17 was the hope of Israel. You cannot divorce the hope and the promise of the resurrection from Old Covenant Israel and her relationship with God, nor can you separate it from Israel's last days. The resurrection does not belong to the end of the Christian age, because the Christian age has no end. It belongs to Israel's last days. Therefore, the resurrection at the end of the millennium occurred by AD 70. Why? Well, because all of God's promises to Old Covenant Israel were fulfilled by AD 70, as James agrees.

Now then, let's talk about something we've touched on just briefly, and that is, Israel and the resurrection. The consummation of Israel's history would be the resurrection at the end of the millennium. We've already seen Acts 24-28, Romans 8, 1 Corinthians 15. All of these are quotations from Old Testament promises. I cannot drive home this point enough. Once we realize that resurrection belongs to Israel and the end of Israel's covenant age, then any concept of a future resurrection, unless Israel remains the chosen people of God, and unless the Old Covenant remains valid today, then any discussion of a future resurrection becomes moot.

All right:
The consummation of Israel's history is confined to the 70 weeks of Daniel 9.
The 70 weeks of Daniel 9 ended in AD 70.
Therefore the consummation of Israel's history, the resurrection at the end of the millennium is confined to the 70 weeks of Daniel, that is, AD 70.

Now I want you to notice something going back to Daniel 9. The consummation of Israel's history would be when sin would be put away. I want you to please catch the power of that. Seventy weeks are determined "to put away sin." All right. Now watch this.

The time of the putting away of sin in fulfillment of God's promises to Israel. 1 Corinthians 15:54-56, is the resurrection at the end of the millennium. But the consummation of Israel's history at the time of the putting away of sin would be at the parousia of Romans 11. Paul, in speaking of the salvation of Israel at the coming of the Lord in fulfillment of Isaiah 27, Isaiah 59, and Jeremiah 31, guess what, would be in AD 70. James has the articles available out there in which he wrote a three-part series in 1991 saying that the parousia of Romans 11:25-27 was fulfilled by AD 70. OK, watch the argument, therefore.

The consummation of Israel's history would be when sin would be put away.

But the time of the putting away of sin in fulfillment of God's promises to Israel is the resurrection at the end of the millennium.

But the consummation of Israel's history at the time of the putting away of sin, Daniel 9, would be at the parousia, the coming of the Lord of Romans, 11.

But James believes that's AD 70.

Therefore, the parousia of Romans 11, verses 25-27, would be the consummation of Israel's history, the time of the resurrection at the end of the millennium, AD 70.

Now let's begin a walk-through Revelation. I understand this is going to be very quick. I understand this is going to move really fast, but especially for those who will get the tapes, I hope you will stop and pause and go to these passages, that you will look at them, that you will examine them very, very carefully. And again, I understand the time constraints put on James by so much material here.

But in Revelation 6, we saw under the altar in the fifth seal, the souls of those who had been beheaded for the cause of Christ. They were given robes which is the defeat of Satan, but they are told to rest for a little while until the fellow brethren who shall be slain as they were should be fulfilled and that day of – when that would be fulfilled, and the answer to their prayer for *vindication*, (the Greek word *ekdekeesis*) how long do you not avenge us that are on the earth would be the day of the Lord of Revelation 6:12f.

Well, I want you to notice Revelation 12, we have the exact same precise elements and motifs. In Revelation 12 we have the birth of the son and the persecution of his seed. But Satan is defeated. Satan is cast out because there is war in heaven between Michael and Satan is cast out. But more suffering is coming because Satan has great wrath knowing that he has only a short time – a micron, a short time, a little time, to persecute the rest of the seed. Guess what the end of that is.

Well, James says, in his Matthew 24 tapes, unless he's changed, and again, I grant that freedom to anybody since I want it myself, but he says in the tapes that was AD 70. Well guess what? The day of the Lord of Revelation 6 is AD 70. James and I agree on that.

What elements do we find therefore in Revelation 20? Revelation 20 the saints that are on the thrones are those that had been under the altar of Revelation 6. But Satan is bound and cast down. But in this period of time at the end of the millennium, more suffering is coming because the nations are gathered together against the Lord and against his host and fire comes down from heaven and destroys them. There's the day of the Lord of Revelation 6 and Revelation 12.

Now Revelation 6 and Revelation 12. I want you to notice, "Suffer a little while, suffer a little while, suffer a little while" in Revelation 6, 12, and 20. Each one of these passages present to us the exact same motifs, the exact same theme, and the exact same time references as well. Therefore, I suggest to you, since the day of the Lord of Revelation 6, and the day of the Lord of Revelation 12, are both AD 70, that demands, unless we can prove otherwise, contextually, that the resurrection of Revelation 20 is disparate and disjunctive from Revelation 6 and Revelation 12 since both of those chapters deal with the coming of the Lord in AD 70, then the coming of the Lord at the end of the millennium resurrection of Revelation 20 was in AD 70.

Okay let's go on just a little bit more. In Revelation 6 and in Revelation 16 we have once again along with Revelation 20, three passages that have exact, precise motifs, themes and time statements. In all three passages, we have the martyrs of God; we have the promise of vindication coming at the day of the Lord. And in all three passages creation is destroyed.

Well, James, as I do, takes Revelation 6, all creation destroyed in AD 70, Revelation 16, Creation destroyed at the judgment of Babylon. James and I agree, that's AD 70 and judgment of Israel and Old Covenant "Babylon." Well, why take Revelation 20? We have a right to demand what is the contextual evidence for delineating between Revelation 20 and Revelation 6 and 16 when the exact same precise language, themes and motifs are present?

Now, could it theocratically be different? Yes. Anybody that's going to be honest with the text has to say, "Yeah, it's possible that we have recurrence, but we have to have proof, not claims. Let's go on just a little bit more.

In Revelation 10 and 11, we have the time of the consummation. John said he heard voices in heaven saying, "The kingdoms of this world had become the kingdoms of our God. He has taken his great power and he has reigned, and the time of the dead that they should be judged has come and the time to reward the prophets." It's the time of the consummation, isn"t it? Isn't the time of the judging of the dead, isn't the time of the rewarding of the prophets, the time of the end, and isn"t that the time of the resurrection? I think so.

Well, what do we have in Revelation 20 at the end of the millennium and the books were opened? And another book was opened and that is the book of life and the dead were judged out of these books and what was that? They were rewarded, right. This is the time of the consummation. In Revelation 10, it's very clearly the resurrection, the time of the dead that they should be judged just like Revelation 20 is the time of the resurrection. Revelation 10 is unequivocally the time of the entrance into the kingdom just as Revelation 21 is the time of the entrance into the everlasting kingdom. Revelation 10 is the time of the rewarding of the dead and the prophets. When was Daniel told that he would be judged? At the time of the end. "Go your way and rest until the time of the end. You shall arise to your inheritance." What's the inheritance? It's the eternal inheritance of verse two.

I won't go into detail in responding to the problem of the "many," but certainly there have been a great, in fact, the great majority of scholars, in spite of the term, "many" in Daniel 12 they believe they it is a prediction of the "final resurrection." I could go into a lot, but I won't take the time to do that at this point.

Nonetheless, Revelation 10 and 11 comes at the time of the judgment of the city where the Lord was slain. It is a direct result of it, just like in Revelation 20, following hard upon the judgment of Babylon, again where the Lord was slain. We have the new Jerusalem, and I would point out that James in the questions that I asked him, I asked him when the new Jerusalem of Revelation 21:2f came, and he said he believed it came in AD 70. Well, if the new Jerusalem of Revelation 21 came in AD 70, that doesn't come until after the millennium of Revelation 20 as we shall show here in just a little bit.

Since I've dealt with Matthew 13, I'm going to go on but I do want to deal with 1 Corinthians 15 and Revelation 14. In 1 Corinthians 15 we have the parousia of Jesus Christ, then comes the end, as it says in verse 21f, which is the time of the harvest of which Jesus is the first fruit. There is the entrance into the kingdom and as we have already seen and emphasized and will continue to emphasize – it is the *telos*, it is the goal, it is the end of the fulfillment of God's promises to Israel. What do we find in Revelation 14.

In Revelation 14 we have the one like the son of man coming on the clouds of heaven and it is the time of the end. It is the time of the harvest of the earth. You see we have to create all sorts of different harvests to dichotomize between 1 Corinthians 15 and Revelation 14. But Revelation 14 and 1 Corinthians 15 are not different because they are both related to the promises God made to Israel. It is entrance into the kingdom, and again, James believes that Revelation 14 was in AD 70. Well, my question again is, how do we delineate? What's the hard exegetical, contextual evidence for delineating between the harvest, the parousia, the end of the age and the kingdom and the fulfillment of Israel's promises in 1 Corinthians 15 and Revelation 14?

Let's go on. In Revelation 15 thru 16, and Revelation 20 and 21, just like in these earlier chapters, we have all these beautiful parallels and harmonies, we find it here as well. In Revelation 15:8f, John said he saw a vision and he saw the ark of the testimony. Heaven was open and he saw the ark of the testimony. My goodness, what an incredible, awesome vision he saw! What would that mean to the good Jewish reader? It means the veil is removed, but John was told no one could enter into the Most Holy Place until the wrath of God was completed. Well, we are told in Revelation 16 in the pouring out of the 7 vials, that the wrath of God would be completed, that 7th vial of God would be poured out – completed. Pay particular attention please that this is the consummation, the finishing of the wrath of God. Okay? God's wrath is finished. When would it occur? When the 7th vial was poured out on the city called Babylon which is where the Lord was slain. When that would happen, when God's wrath was completed, in the pouring out of vengeance on Babylon, entrance into the Most Holy Place would occur. By the way, the writer of Hebrews, Hebrews 9, which also happens to be one of my favorite verses, I'll guarantee you, Ward.

Entrance into the Most Holy Place is not yet made manifest while that first tabernacle has validity, not while it's still standing physically while it still has validity is the power of the Greek text, and that Old Testament system stood in divers ordinances imposed on them until the time of reformation. Take the validity of the Old C system out of the way, and you have access to the most Holy place. Thus, at the end of the Old C age, entrance into the Most Holy Place would be open to man. Which agrees perfectly with Revelation 16 because judgment on Babylon would result in the opening of the Most Holy Place, allowing entrance into it.

Now watch what happens in Revelation 20 and 21. The new creation of Revelation 21 most assuredly and chapter 22 as well equals the Most Holy Place. In his book, *The Garden of God*, James iterates that very well – beautifully, as matter of fact, I think. But when would that entrance into that Most Holy Place of Revelation 21 and 22 take place? At the end of the millennium when heaven and earth is destroyed. But the new heaven and new earth is only created, Revelation 21 when the first heaven and earth has passed away. But again, that only occurs at the end of the millennium. In other words entrance into that Most Holy Place of Revelation 21 and 22 only occurs when? After the vengeance at the end of the millennium takes place. In other words the wrath is completed at the end of the millennium.

That means that entrance into the Most Holy Place, entrance into the new creation comes at the end of the millennium. But entrance into the Most Holy Place would take place when God's wrath was completed. God's wrath was completed in the destruction of Jerusalem. Therefore, the new creation at the end of the millennium was at the destruction of Jerusalem in AD 70. Here's the argument: Entrance into the most holy is entrance into the new creation, but entrance into the new creation is after the millennium. Because the new creation only comes after the destruction of the old, but the destruction of the old Israel is at the end of the millennium. The entrance into the Most Holy Place occurs at the end of the Mosaic age. That's what Hebrews 9:10, says. Therefore the end of the millennium is at the end of the Mosaic Age, not the end of the Christian Age. You mean to tell me that we still don't have access to the Most Holy Place today?

We've already discussed Daniel 12. He and I agree on Daniel 12, but I think it's important to see it – well, let's go back and do it anyway. Daniel 12 we have the time of the end when the book of life would be opened and those written there would be saved which is the time of the resurrection and that's AD70. He and I agree on that.

What happens in Revelation 20 through 22? It is the time of the end when the book of life is opened. Folks listen to me, do a study of the book of life in the ot. Book of life belonged to Israel. It was Israel's book of life. It was the time of the resurrection and what did Jesus say about the judgment in which he would come to judge all men? "Behold, I come quickly and my reward is with me."

Okay, I want you to follow the argument. The new heavens and the new earth, that is the new creation, was an Old Testament promise made to Israel. Listen to me, please, you can not delineate, just like resurrection, just like redemption, just like salvation, just like taking away sin. You cannot divorce those promises from God's promises to Israel. You can't do it. The new heavens and the new earth. The new creation was an Old Testament promise made to Israel. Isaiah 65. When did Isaiah say the new heavens and new earth would come?

Isaiah 65:13, "I will destroy you," speaking of Old Covenant Israel, "and I will call my people by a new name, my servant shall sing, but you will cry for sorrow apart, for behold I created a new heavens and new earth, and I create Jerusalem a blessing."

The new heavens and new earth would only come when Israel was destroyed. Well, all promises made to Israel were fulfilled by AD 70. James agrees. Therefore the promise of the new heavens and new earth, the new creation, was fulfilled by AD 70. Listen to me again. We're not talking here in Revelation 20, 21,and 22 about a typological new creation. We're talking about the ultimate new creation, and it was the promise that God made to Israel. So let me emphasize and reiterate that no matter how many passing of heaven and earth we might see in the ot, which I do, and agree with James, no matter how many new creations we may have seen created, all of those were typological pointing to the ultimate, consummation that would occur at the end of Israel's age, not at the end of the Christian age. You cannot divorce the soteriological, the messianic, and the eschatological promises from Israel without violating biblical eschatology.

Okay, the new creation promise was fulfilled in AD70 because it was a promise made to Israel, but the new creation would arrive at the end of the millennium (Revelation 20:11f), Destruction of Old Creation (Revelation 20:11-12), New Creation (Revelation 21:1f). But the New Creation would arrive at the end of the millennium. Again, therefore, the end of the millennium would arrive in AD70.

Now, we all agree, James and I certainly agree, that death would be destroyed, whatever we want to mean by that term, all right? At the end of the millennium, 1 Corinthians 15, Revelation 20. But I want you to notice something. Revelation 21:2-3 says, that in this New Jerusalem, there is no more death. But James says in *The Garden of God* and *Through New Eyes* that the New Jerusalem – and by the way, he said that in response to my written questions to him as well – the New Jerusalem came in AD70. Therefore, the end of the millennium, when death was destroyed, and the New Jerusalem in which there is no death, came in AD70.

I want to touch upon Revelation 19 and 21 because these two passages talk about the wedding of the lamb. The wedding of Revelation 19 and 21 would be at the time of the judgment of Babylon, but it's also at the end of the millennium. You see in Revelation 19, "Rejoice and be glad, for the time of the wedding is come." Well what is Revelation 21, "I saw the new Jerusalem adorned as a bride for her husband descending out of God for what? For the wedding. Therefore, the parousia, against Babylon, is at the end of the millennium.

Now I want to take note of something here. James says, in his tape series, "The AD70 Heresy," that he did in 1999, Tape 9A, and again he may have changed his views on this, and we'll gladly hear what he has to say. But he said, the wedding ceremony is something that takes place between AD30 and AD70. And he also said, "We are in the time of the wedding feast now, and the wedding takes place at the end of the feast." I believe that to be critically, critically wrong. Arland Hultgren, in his relatively new book, entitled The Parables of Jesus, says, and does really ,a long extended and in depth examination of the Jewish wedding practices, says, "The second stage, that is after the betrothal, was the marriage itself," now watch, number 3, "followed by the wedding feast." In other words, the feast followed the wedding. Folks, we're not waiting for the wedding. If we are, what kind of sons and daughters are we?

But notice this. Please catch the power of this. The promise of the wedding is the promise made to Old Covenant Israel. Remember that Paul said in Romans 15:8, that this I testify that Jesus Christ became a servant to the circumcision to confirm the promises made to the fathers. What was one of Jesus' favorite themes? The wedding feast. Where did Jesus get the promise, the idea, the theme and motif of the wedding feast? He got it out of Isaiah 62 after saying in Isaiah 42 and Isaiah 49 of how Israel had been forsaken, God predicted in Isaiah 62 that the time was coming in which God said, "you will no longer be called abandoned and forsaken, but you shall be called *hephsivah*, and Buelah.

You know when we sing the song, Buelah Land, do you know what that means? Married. Why? Because God said I'm going to marry you again. In Hosea and that's actually chapter 2:19, after divorcing Israel and saying that Old Covenant form of Israel would never rise again

Hosea 1:5, God said that the time was coming in which I will betroth you again to me in righteousness. God said you're going to be my bride again. The promise of the wedding belonged to Israel.

Well, again, James says, all of God's promises were fulfilled by AD70. I agree with that. Therefore, the promise of the wedding of Rev. 19, the promise of the wedding rev. 21 was fulfilled by AD70. Well the wedding was in Ad70 but the wedding occurs at the end of the millennium, Revelation 21:2-7; therefore the end of the millennium was in AD70.

Very, very quickly, I want you to notice that Jesus said in Matthew 16:27-28, a passage, I think, that James and I agree on, we have the promise of the coming of the Lord and the judgment of all men before all of those people died. In Rev. 22, Jesus reiterates that promise and says, "Behold, I come quickly, and my reward is with me to judge all men." What did he say, behold I come quickly. Now watch this.

The judgment of all men is the time of the resurrection.

But the judgment of all men was near when John wrote Rev 22:12.

Therefore the resurrection at the end of the millennium was near when John wrote.

What have we seen? We have seen from *analogia scriptura*, that the end of the millennium was in AD70. We have seen that the link between Israel and resurrection is absolutely inextricable. We have seen the emphatic time statements of the parousia and the judgment prove that the end of the millennium was near. We have seen the consistent testimony of Revelation that proves that the end of the millennium was near. I suggest again that we have demonstrated our proposition. Thank you.

James Jordan's Second Negative

What I would like to do in this half hour is to continue on where I left off with some pre-suppositional material, and then in the last segment maybe I can try to prove to you the millennium didn't end in AD 70. And engage a bit. But, let me continue on with this and challenge you along these lines.

We were talking about contexts, and the first context that I suggested is that, warts and all, the tradition of the church has to be strongly respected whenever we start to come up with things that seem to deviate. This doesn't mean you can't question; doesn't mean that everything's going to come out exactly the way it ever has been; doesn't mean that the new ideas are wrong; just means that there should be a hermeneutics of carefulness about these things.

The second thing I've tried to argued with you is the physicality of the biblical world view, and the third thing I would like to give you to start talking about is the philosophy of history, where the point is that the Adamic history as a context for Israel's history. And I'll get at that indirectly, and I imagine talk about it some tomorrow as well.

So what does the Bible teach about the goal of history? To begin with we have to admit that God has chosen to present teaching about the nature of the world and the goal of history for the most part through symbolic and typological form. Like it or not, understand it or not, know it or not, the Bible is front-loaded with a vast amount of symbolic and ritual instruction that is designed to shape the understanding of those who live into it.

The last half of Exodus, all of Leviticus, about half of Numbers are given over to this. Precious little of this material is explained. The people were simply told to live in terms of it and gradually their living by these symbolic rules would shape their thinking and they would begin to understand it. Having laid this foundation, the Bible continues to add to it. Virtually all the narratives that come afterwards allude to various parts of all this symbolic, ritual typological material. The Psalms are full of allusions to it as David had been shaped by it. With the temple we have another dump of symbolic material in the temple itself, and in the descriptions of it's new furniture. And the book of Canticles is written in terms of it with the groom portrayed in temple language and the bride in language taken from the land.

Yet another large dump of symbolic material comes from the books of Ezekiel, Daniel, and Zechariah, all of which comes from and transforms symbolism found in the tabernacle, temple, and other symbolic parts of the earlier scriptures. But how well is this understood, even today? How many expositors of the book of Daniel think that the four metals in the great image of the temple come from Greek notions about an age of gold and an age of silver and an age of bronze and an age of iron? Instead of seeing that they come from the temple, which has gold in the holy of holies, a ring of silver around that, bronze items out in the courtyard and iron all over the outer gates. Very clear. This is related to the temple.

How many recognize in Daniel 3, that the pillar at one end of this courtyard, the furnace at the other, and the orchestra is all a parody of Levitical temple worship and would instantly have been recognized as such by an ancient Jew reading the passage? How many recognize that Daniel 7 is built on Ezekiel 1-3 – very clearly? And behind that on the ritual of the Day of Atonement in Leviticus 16 in which the high priest ascends to God in heavenly, most holy incense clouds and receives the kingdom anew in glorious garments. It's not recognized. The book of Daniel is not understood this way because it's not taken in the context in which it is written.

So if we're not very familiar with the Bible's earlier symbolic presentations, we're not going to see what's there in these later passages and we'll not be in a good position to grasp the symbolic prophetic passages in the New Testament. I'm sure we all agree with that. God also shaped the understanding of his people through narratives and through rituals that are but encoded narratives. The ritual of Leviticus 1, for instance, replays the exodus from Egypt and the arrival at Sinai, restoring those who have fallen back into a spiritual Egypt to the presence of God. Both the narratives and the rituals of the Bible are almost all death and resurrection stories of various sorts. And that's what I want to talk about for a few minutes here.

I want to talk about the fact that God is a god who takes things into forms of death and then back out into more glorified forms of resurrection, and he does that, sin or no sin. In Genesis 1 evenings give way to mornings with each new day bringing a new and more glorious physical world. This is where the Bible begins. It's the first thing we learn – that new days do not take place in some other location but are glorified versions of the old place. That God glorifies the original physical world. We are not led to believe that glory means moving out of this world but that this world is glorified, externally, visibly, tangibly.

Following upon this in Genesis 2, the man is glorified after being put into death sleep. While in this coma, he's ripped in half. He wasn't just asleep, folks -- you pull a bone out of somebody while they're asleep, they'll wake up. This is a different word. It's the word *tardemah*. It's not related to the word for sleep. It always means death-sleep. We'll come back to it a little bit later on. But it's in this place that God makes covenants with people, in Genesis 15 and other places – it's a form of death.

While he's in this death-like situation, he's torn in half, but then he wakes up to a new world. He wakes up glorified because the woman is the glory of a man, as Paul says. Therefore, to add a woman is to glorify Adam. It has nothing to do with sin, going into this death-like situation and coming out of it. It's not because he's a sinner and has to be forgiven. It's because this is what God does. He takes the world from glory to glory. He takes people from glory to glory. Sin was just a spanner into the works. This is nothing less than a new physical existence for Adam. His body is different. Adam as a whole is now two different kinds of people.

Others are also are put into death-sleep. Abram is put into death-sleep in Genesis 15 and is told that after 400 hundred years the famine-plagued land of promise will be glorified into a land flowing with milk and honey. A new glorified world. Jonah goes into death-sleep and arises to bring death and resurrection to Assyria, and they go into mourning and then they become a new Nineveh.

In Daniel 10-12, Daniel goes into death-sleep and he's shown the tribulation of the Jews in the coming age of which his own death-sleep is a type, and also the eventual resurrection of the Jews from dust to glory when Messiah comes, of which his own lifting up from the dust by the angel is a type.

We're going back to Adam. Adam is told that in the day he eats of the tree of knowledge he will die. But he's also told that every tree shall be food for him and Eve. Eventually then he most assuredly will eat of the tree of the knowledge of good and evil and he will die when he is ready. We shall return to what this means later on, but for now, we can see that Adam knew what this would mean, practically speaking, for when he went into death-sleep his body was changed and he arose to glory. This is what would have happened if he had waited for God's permission to eat of the tree of knowledge -- something like this, we don't know exactly what, but some type of transformation of his life.

I shall argue that he would need to do this in order to acquire the ability to deal with Satan. And since Satan is an angel and Adam is made lower than the angels, he had no power to deal with this angelic invader of the Garden. In order to deal with the holy war, he would need to go through good-death, whatever that would have been like, and been raised with the power to deal with angels, raised up over the angels, higher than the angels, which of course is what's happened to us. In Jesus we now battle principalities and powers. Nobody in the Old Testament could. You don't find people in the Old Testament having to deal with demons. They couldn't; they had not been given this experience that Jesus goes through for us and then gives us the benefit of.

Speaking of deaths and resurrections though, there are numerous exoduses in the Bible – Noah from the old world, Abram from Ur, Jacob from Paddan-aram, Israel from Egypt, the Ark from Philistia, loaded up with golden mice and golden emerods, the Jews from Babylon, and many others. What are these but death and resurrection events of another sort? In each case the spoils from the dead and judged world are transformed into the glorious features of the new world. These are just more extended versions of evenings and mornings where what you come to after the evening, after the night of difficulty, is better. Though sin has made evenings more intense, joy comes in the morning, and the world's different.

In the narratives of the Old Testament, covenants are made which are then broken. The people go into various kinds of bondage or exile, but the older covenant is never restored. Rather a new covenant is made, one that is a glorified form of the old, and which involves elevating the people to higher and higher rule over the world. Noah was made a world king able to deal with things he could not have dealt with before the flood. Abram was given preliminary dominion over the land. At Sinai Israel was made a nation of priests and given a law that would be a light to the nations around about – expansion of influence. The Davidic covenant with the glorious temple glorified Israel, further enhancing her witness. With the restoration after the exile Israel was relieved of the burden of maintaining an army to guard herself and was granted even more power as a nation of prophets spread out throughout the *oikoumene*.

All of these are death and resurrection events. In fact, once you begin to understand it and to watch for this, there really aren't any stories in the Old Testament that aren't about some kind of death and resurrection. It may not be sin, it may just be something God puts his people through in order to train them, but it involves stepping back, it involves going through an evening, it involves going through a transition, a transition at midnight. How many midnight transitions are there in the Old Testament? How many are there in the book of Acts? On the ship. Eutychus.

But there's another kind of death and resurrection narrative found in the scriptures. Individual dead corpses are brought to life again. To be sure, these people were not glorified and eventually died again, but these events are part of what formed the world view of the Jews. Consider how these things add up. God is a god who makes vast changes in the physical world that he created, glorifying it through evenings and new days; big changes; physical changes in the configuration of the universe during that first week. God is a god who puts Adam to sleep into an evening, changes his body, and glorifies him. God is a god who takes his people through a variety of social and personal death and resurrection experiences which always result in new glory. God is a god who brings dead people back to life in physical bodies.

Now, I submit to you that it's not hard to see how all this information would lead the Jews to believe that the god who does these things will eventually raise up physically dead people in new and glorified bodies in a new and glorified world. I submit that the traditional understanding of texts like in Job – "with these eyes I shall see" – fits with this. But there's considerable more data that bears on this matter.

For instance, the laws of cleansing. The word unclean basically means symbolically dead. This is because all the various kinds of uncleanness come from dead things of various sorts. Death spreads. Paul says, death spreads to all men. We always think of that in terms of generations, but it's also true in terms of these symbolical laws. Uncleanness - symbolic death - spreads from one person to another. That's the way it is under the law. Contact with dead animal carcasses. Eating animals positioned in part of the realm of the dead in various ways. Blood inside the body is life, but flowing away in death from the center of the human body in the various issues causes uncleanness. Dead skin on a person that reveals the flesh underneath. And most potently contact or even near proximity to the human corpse.

Cleansing is with living water and hence means resurrection. It's more than a little interesting that the ritual for resurrecting a person who contracts death from a human corpse involves baptismal resurrection on the third day and then again on the seventh day according to Numbers 19. I think this is an important passage. I'm certain that one could be a consistent preterist and force this passage to fit the consistent preterist view. But I do want to at least call your attention to it because it's one of the clearest places where you've got a double resurrection.

Somehow or other that needs to be factored in as something that the Jews understand, especially the priests. They do this all the time. Hear Numbers 19 verse 12, "The one who shall purify himself from uncleanness with the water," this is ash, heifer ash in water, "on the third day and on the seventh day, he shall be clean. If he does not purify himself on the third day and on the seventh day, he shall not be clean." You have introduced into the thinking of Israel a double resurrection – one on the third day and a more complete second resurrection on the seventh. This kind of two stage resurrection is also seen in the restoration of the leper in Leviticus 14. I'll let you look at that on your own, but you've got two stages there.

In both cases, there is a partial resurrection followed by a full one. And I submit to you that this is the thinking that underlies the two resurrections of which Jesus spoke in John 5. After all, I have to refer to John 5, don't I? Let me just read it and remind you of what it saith. "Truly, truly, I say to you," this is John 5:24-29, "I say to you, he who hears my word and believes him who sent me has eternal life and does not come into judgment but is passed out of death into life." Here he's not talking about some event in AD70 or anything else historical. It's very much sort of the pietist notion: believe in Jesus and you've moved out of death into life. You don't even go through judgment. So this is one kind of resurrection here. "Truly, truly I say to you an hour is coming and now is when the dead shall hear the voice of the Son of God and those who hear shall live for just as the Father has life in Himself, even so he gave to the Son also to have life in Himself and He gave Him the authority to execute judgement because He is the Son of Man." He is the greater Ezekiel.

Now we understand this to be some kind of spiritual resurrection, coming back to life again. Verse 28, "Do not marvel at this for an hour is coming," and he does not say *and now is*, "in which all who are in the tombs shall hear His voice and shall come forth, those who did good deeds to a resurrection of life and those who committed evil to a resurrection of judgment."

Now consider the thinking informed by these rituals that went on all the time in Judaism, such as leprosy and corpse contamination. There's nothing sinful about being contaminated by a corpse. Someone dies; you've got to take care of them. You've got to bury them; you've got to come into the room and give them one last kiss on the forehead or whatever, but you're unclean for a week, and you've got to do this ashes of the heifer water thing on the third and seventh day. Everybody was doing this all the time; they all knew about double resurrections. So with this thinking informed by these rituals that went on all the time, Jesus' hearers would not think of the two resurrections of which He spoke as the same event.

And believing as they did in an eventual physical resurrection and the final judgment of all men, which was the common belief among the Jews at the time, it would not occur that Jesus meant anything other than first, a soteriological resurrection, followed eventually by a physical one. Such, I submit, is the case. And indeed, Jesus' reference to a physical resurrection from the tomb is followed up in John with the resurrection of Lazarus who came to life in his tomb precisely in the way Jesus describes here by hearing Jesus' voice. Lazarus was only one man and his raising can only be a type of what He predicts, which applies to all. He says, "All who are in the tombs shall hear the voice of the Son of Man," Jesus' voice, "and shall come forth." I find it difficult with this context and background and with the example of Lazarus in here to see this as other than a second resurrection after the first, and one that is physical in nature along the traditional lines.

That doesn't explain how I'm going to get around the fact that all these promises are for Israel and I am going to get around that, but I think I will get around that later. This will be a good place to stop. Basically what I shall argue is that Israel's history is like a parenthesis within the larger Adamic history and there is an eschatology implied in the early chapters of Genesis that overarches Israel's history. Israel is a new Adam, specifies it, and they have a history that deals with redemption and the holy war around that. There is an implied larger history so that the promises that are for Israel are actually for everybody, for all men if you look back in the Adamic direction. That will be the form of the argument that I shall make later on, but I'll stop here for now.

Don K. Preston's Third Affirmative

All right. Let me begin here I've got 25 minutes, and I do want to respond to some of the things that James has said. And you know, an awful lot of what he has to say is very fascinating, but I would also suggest that in a way it is irrelevant because, if Paul and Peter and the New Testament writers posit the ultimate eschatological end of the millennium resurrection at the end of Israel's age, then to even suggest that there was another eschatology other than that says that this resurrection for which Israel was longing, that Paul talked about in 1 Corinthians 15, that was the ultimate resurrection. Well is that not the ultimate resurrection suggested in Genesis, 2? I would suggest that there are not two eschatologies. I would suggest rather that the promise in Genesis 2, is that which is magnified and defined in the promises made to Israel and brought to their consummation at the end of Israel's age.

James has raised an issue and hinted; he hasn't accused, I want to be clear about that, but he has hinted that perhaps, we as preterists, believe that creation is somehow evil. Well, I don't. I'm not Epicurean, thankfully. Nor am I Stoic. I tried to be Stoic when they pulled a tooth and it didn't work really well. But, nonetheless, I don't believe that creation is inherently evil. I just believe that there is something, in fact, that is better. I will make the statement that I heard Max King make years ago – that after I pass from this life, I believe that I will have a somatic existence. I don't believe that the Bible tells me a whole lot about it. I am absolutely 100% convinced that when I leave this body, I am going to enter an existence that Paul, who was not a gnostic, even though one scholar called Paul a gnostic. Nonetheless that Paul who said, "I have a desire to depart and be with Christ which is far better."

You know, as good as this life is, and God made a wonderful world., and I love this life. I love my human relationships; I love my wife, I love my kids – well, most of the time, I love my kids – but anyway, you understand the point that I'm making. No, I don't despise this world. I simply believe that God's scheme of redemption has something that is "far better." And there are many other passages that I can allude to on that so I don't want any misunderstanding.

I certainly don't want to be accused of being a gnostic in the sense of anyone suggesting that we believe that this physical body is evil. I do believe with all my heart, and this needs to be understood by anyone and everyone who listens and watches this tape, I personally don't know, I've heard of some, but I don't know for a fact, of preterists who say that this physical body or this physical creation is evil. Now we could go to Romans 8, where Paul says, "God sent forth his son in the likeness of sinful flesh." And we can talk about it. But Paul was not a gnostic in that text, but I would accept, nonetheless, what he had to say.

All right, let me make sure I've covered some things– everything that I wanted to say. Okay, he brought up Acts 17, therefore let me go to Acts 17 and take note of some things from this passage. In Acts, Paul said God has appointed, He's designated, He's cut out a time, a day, in which He is about to judge the world in righteousness. Now I want to make this statement. It really makes no difference how we define the *oikoumene* in Acts 17, all right? It doesn't' matter if we define it as the Jewish *oikoumene* or the Roman *oikoumene*. The bottom line is that Acts 17 is the ultimate eschatological end of the millennium resurrection and Paul says God has appointed a day in which he is "about to."

Now he uses the Greek word, *mello*, in the infinitive. Blass-DeBrunner says that *mello* with the infinitive indicates imminence, Furthermore, nearly all the Greek lexicons, in fact, basically, all Greek lexicons – I only know of one that tries to negate it, and they do a real poor job of it I might add . But, nonetheless, Thayer says that *mello* with the infinitive means to be about to do something. The infinitive means to be on the point of doing something.

Arndt and Gingrich agrees. Vines agrees. Analytical Greek Lexicon agrees. So if we take *mello* in its normal translation of about to be, and by the way, it's absolutely fascinating to see how the translators deal, or I should say, maybe really don't deal with *mello*. We'll find that it is used in context of imminency.

Furthermore, let me have the next chart, 35C. Let's take a look at the word, *oikoumene*. I think it's very important for us to see something. Jesus said, "This gospel of the kingdom will preached in all the

world," *oikoumene*. Well, do we take that Jewish or do we take that Roman? It doesn't matter. Watch this.
The "Whole World."
Mt. 24:14-preached in All World- *(Holos Oikoumene)*
Lk. 2:1-whole World to Be Taxed- (Pasan Oikoumene)
Ax 11:28--famine over Whole World- (Holos Oikoumene)
Ax 17:31-judge the World–(Oikoumene)
Rev. 3:10-trial Coming on Whole World– (Holos Oikoumene)

Jordan (Matthew 24, Tape 2, Side 2)—> Romans 1; Colossians 1:8 "You Can Plug in Whatever 'World' You Want, 'Entire Known World'; 'Entire Civilized World'; or Whatever, but Whatever You Plug in There You Have to Plug into Matthew 24."

Luke 2:1- Caesar Augustus passed an edict that "the whole world," obviously the Roman world under his control. It wasn't South America. In Acts 11, there was to be a famine that was to come over the whole world, *oikoumene*, (Acts 17:31) our present text. And in Revelation 3:10, Jesus said, speaking to the church at Philadelphia, "I will keep you from the tribulation that is about to come on the whole *oikoumene*.

I want you to notice something. As Matthew 24 states, on side two, in discussing Romans 1 and Colossians 1:8, James says, "You can plug in whatever 'world' you want, entire known world, entire civilized world, or whatever, but whatever you plug in there, you have to plug into Matthew 24. Well, I agree. I believe that's consistency of language.

So, if you plug Acts 17, the *oikoumene* of Acts 17, into Matthew 24, when would the judgment of Matthew 24 and the *oikoumene* of Matthew 24 occur? "Verily, I say unto you, this generation shall not pass until all these things be fulfilled" (Matthew 24:34).

Furthermore, next chart, James and I certainly agree that the judgment of Acts 17 is the end of the millennium resurrection judgment. We both agree with that. Well, let me emphasize this. That is, the judgment resurrection of Acts 17 is the time of the fulfillment of the promises made to Israel. I've said this before – I'm going to say it again, several times probably, during this debate. You cannot separate Paul's eschatology from the eschatology of Israel.

Paul's eschatology was the eschatology of Israel. And let me reiterate a point I made just at the beginning of this third speech, and that is, if you say that Israel's eschatology was not the eschatology of Genesis 2, then Paul was wrong in 1 Corinthians 15 to posit that resurrection, and that of 1 Thessalonians 4 as Israel's eschatology, and to say his doctrine of the resurrection, his promise of the end of the millennium resurrection was in fact the hope of Israel. If Genesis 2 and 3 have a different eschatology then 1 Thessalonians 4 and 1 Corinthians 15 which are Israel's eschatology, then what is 1 Thessalonians 4, and 1 Corinthians 15?

You see, we're forced to ask these questions. Furthermore, I would remind you that on his tapes James did say that the entire Adamic world of Genesis 2 and 3, therefore the eschatology of Genesis 2 and 3 occurred in AD 70.

Let me go on a bit further. He made the comment and he made the comment on Acts 17, but let me try to drive this home. He said the New Testament is concerned with the end of Israel, true, but with Rome, as well. Well, let me reiterate – if you try to make that Acts 17, it really doesn't matter because Paul said it was near. He said it was about to happen. But if you dichotomize between Acts 17 and say that's the destruction of Rome, then where are you going to place Israel's eschatology? Israel's eschatology is final eschatology. So, if Israel's eschatology, the resurrection at the end of the millennium, is the ultimate eschatology, then guess what, you've got to have Rome's eschatology before the final eschatology of Israel. You cannot dichotomize and divide those up in that particular way.

Let me go on here and make sure I'm getting this. James alluded and he said, "Christian teaching has always taught the restoration of creation even of animals."Well, I think we're dealing here with a problem of tradition, aren't we? How valid is tradition? Now, I want James to know and I want anyone else to know, I don't just take with a blanket hand and summarily dismiss all of history and tradition. I read the church fathers. I appreciate much, but there's an awful lot, I don't have a problem in the world, to be honest about it, when I read the patristic or when I read the apostolic writers and church fathers, I have no problem whatsoever, when they go to a passage, and they very clearly, undeniably, irrefutably violate the context and the emphatic statements of scriptures. You know what? I don't have a problem saying, Iranaeus was wrong, Apollonius, was wrong, well whatever you want to think of Apollonius. I don't have a problem when I read those individuals, and they're so clearly out of step with emphatic statements of scripture, I don't have a problem stepping back and going, you know what, they were wrong.

Even when I go to Eusebius, as respected as he is, when I go to him and read some of his comments, I'm going, wow! Sorry, Eusebius, you were wrong. I don't care how many of the ensuing Christians followed him; he's still wrong. James made the comment, which I absolutely agree with, just because history has stood and tradition has stood, that does not mean that we do not have a right to challenge it. Isn't that what Martin Luther did? And he also stated that it doesn't prove that the new ideas are wrong. Well, thank God, because that would mean that Martin Luther was automatically wrong, wouldn't it? No, I agree with James in this 100% when he says the tradition of the church must be honored, okay that's fine. But I firmly believe in *sola scriptura.*

James even says on one of his tapes in regard to 2 Thessalonians 2, and the man of sin that the creeds have had to be altered and modified from time to time to bring them into closer harmony with the understanding, that it's not the pope. I respect Martin Luther. In fact, he's one of my heroes. I love Martin Luther. But Martin Luther said the pope is the anti-christ and the man of sin. He had a whole lot of other ugly things that I can't say in public about the man of sin. Well, okay. I respect and admire an awful lot of them.

As Sam quoted one scholar: "We are standing on the shoulders of giants. We are midgets standing on the shoulders of giants." But you know what, if the giant is wrong in some aspects, then I need to have the courage and the insight and the willingness to say, Brother Luther, I believe you were wrong, and here's why.

James did ask the question, what is the goal of history? Would you get your Bible and follow along with me right here? What is the goal of history? Is it the end of the Christian age? Is it the re-creation of material creation? Paul in 1 Corinthians 10:11 said, after giving several examples of sin and rebellion and God's punishment against Old Covenant Israel, said, "These things happen unto them as examples unto us on whom the end of the ages has come." Well, I'd like for us to take just a little bit closer look at that. Because Paul uses the Greek word, *telos*. I don't have to tell any of you that have looked into the Greek that *telos* can mean termination. That's true it can. But most of the time it means, goal, end, destiny. Paul what are you saying to us? Paul says here's what I'm saying, the goal of all previous ages has *katantao*, arrived, reached its destiny. What is the goal of the age? It's not the end of the Christian age. It's the arrival and consummation of the body of Christ, the church of the living God because Paul living then and having his part, his ministry, in transforming that world from the Old Covenant world of sin and death to the world of life and righteousness said, the goal of all previous ages has arrived, has come upon us. That's powerful stuff and I think answers the question very well.

And James went through some examples of typological death and resurrection. I agree with everyone of those, by the way. Adam died, woman came forth, man was glorified in woman, Abraham died, Jonah died. Daniel died. I agreed with all of those. But the question is: What do they typify? Do they for foreshadow a physical resurrection? I would suggest that James' paradigm turns 1 Corinthians 15:46 on its head. I would suggest to you that types go from the physical to the spiritual. Paul said that God's *modus operandi*, that which is spiritual is not first. But that which is natural and then the spiritual.

What is James' paradigm? Well, it's exactly the one that I used to hold. That is, we've been spiritually resurrected, now we're waiting on physical resurrection. No, that's not Paul's concept. Paul said that which is natural is first, then the spiritual. I would suggest to you that all these examples of the Old Testament, these typological examples, did not foreshadow a physical resurrection. These physical events that happened to them foreshadowed the coming spiritual resurrection of which Christ would be the first fruit. Christ was the first one raised from the dead. He wasn't the first one raised from physical death. He was the first raised from the death of Adam. Sin death. And we follow that.

I think it is important for us therefore, to discuss the nature of the death which Adam died. God told Adam, in the day, he didn't say 900 years later, nor did he say you will begin to die. The Hebrew of the text is, according to those who know Hebrew, in dying, you shall die. It's not two deaths – one death.

In Genesis 20:7-17, Abimelech was going to take Sarai and God appeared to Abimelech and said if you touch the woman you will surely die. In dying you will die. Now what kind of death was he threatening him with? I know what kind of death He was threatening him with. He was threatening him with physical death, there's no doubt about it. But you know what, back here in Genesis 2, God said, "In the day you eat," -- now, let there be no mistake whatsoever about the meaning of "in the day you eat, you shall surely die."

If you want to see the meaning of that go to Numbers 30 and you will see case after case after case in which that term and throughout the Old Testament really, in which God said, "in the day" you do this, or you do that, this is going to happen, and it didn't mean 900 years later. And it doesn't mean you'll begin to, it doesn't mean you'll come under the sentence of, it means the day you do it, here's what's going to happen. Could we cite an example or two that might be exceptions? Well that might possibly be, but we're looking at the consistency of scripture in this particular situation.

I also find it fascinating, and I happen to agree to a certain extent with what James had to say. James said, and James I want to make sure I get this correctly. You feel free to correct this when you get back up, but in your writings you indicate that prior to sinning, man would have transitioned from this world any way. He said he would have had to pass through, "good death." And in the tapes that James has produced, he has definitely said that man would die, that his transition from this world into heaven itself, had he not sinned. It was the entrance of death that put the sting into death, made death bad. Well, I agree with that, if you want to use that terminology. Well let's take a look at that.

Death, physical death, let's use this terminology, physical death without sin has no sting. Let's approach it from that point. If sin is what made it bad for Adam to transition, because after all, Adam's sin alienated him from God, did it not? Separated him. Therefore, when Adam died physically because of his sin, he doesn't get to go to heaven where he would have had he not sinned, according to James and me both. So sin's the problem.

Chart 49a.
From What Death Did Hosea Predict Resurrection?
Hosea. 13:1--when Israel Sinned She Died! –Assyrian Captivity!–
Sin-death/separation from Presence of God!

Isaiah 24:4f– They Have Violated the Everlasting Covenant
Is. 27:7-8--Israel Slain by Being Sent Away!
Ezekiel. 37:11–Israel Dead When in Captivity--sin Death!

Jordan (Matthew 24: Tape 1) "When the NT Uses OT. Citations We must Go to the OT to See What it Meant in the OT. We Interpret the Bible by Comparing Scripture with Scripture!" (EOC)

I want you to notice that Paul said in 1 Corinthians 15, "As in Adam all men die, even so in Christ shall all be made alive." Paul said that the resurrection that he was talking about, 1 Corinthians 15, would overcome the death introduced by Adam. The great question is what death is he talking about. Well it's the death of Adam, the day you eat, you shall surely die. Did they die physically? No, they didn't. Furthermore, Paul said that the resurrection would be when these two passages were fulfilled, Hosea 13:1. Now James says in some of his tapes that when a New Testament writer quotes from an Old Testament prophet, we need to go back there to the Old Testament and determine from the context what he's talking about. Couldn't agree more with that. Absolutely could not agree more with that.

Okay, what kind of death is Hosea 13:1 and verse 13 and 14 talk about? Notice, Hosea 13:1: When Israel sinned, she died. How? By going into Assyrian captivity. You have sin, death and separation from God, as W. D. Davies says, that Israel in the land was alive, but Israel outside the land was dead. So what happened with Israel? She's outside of the land, she's dead; when she's brought back into the land, resurrection. I agree.

All right. Isaiah 24:4f, Israel violated the everlasting covenant. Israel, in 27:7-9 was slain by being sent away. But in Ezekiel 37:11 Israel died when she was in captivity. All of these, you see, are similar concept. But here's the point, it's not physical death, is it? God was promising to bring Israel back into covenant relationship with her to restore her to his presence. That was the resurrection being promised.

Now I want you to notice what James says about hermeneutics. When the New Testament uses Old Testament citations, we must go to the Old Testament and see what it meant in the Old Testament. We interpret the Bible by comparing scripture with scripture. Amen. Hallelujah. All right. Paul was anticipating the final eschatological end of the millennium resurrection in fulfillment of Hosea 13 and Isaiah 25:8. But you can't find physical death or resurrection in Isaiah 25:8 or in Hosea 13. Israel was separate from the land, divorced from God. And thus, dead. Go to the next chart. (Chart number unknown).

Once again, let's take a look at this. Paul says that resurrection, and I must emphasize this again, this was end of the millennium resurrection. Whatever James wants to say about an eschatology of Genesis 2 and 3, let me reiterate again, in his tapes he said that the law, the world of Genesis 2 and 3 came to an end in AD70. So that's AD 70 eschatology.

Well, okay, Paul in 1 Corinthians 15 is not dealing with a different eschatology than Genesis 2 and 3 because in Genesis 2 and 3 he's talking about the destruction of Satan. The overcoming of the death that was introduced by Satan. That's what Paul's talking about in 1 Corinthians 15. So the law, the sin and the death of Genesis 2 and 3 is what Paul is talking about to be overcome at the time of the fulfillment of God's promises to Israel. Again, it's not a different eschatology in Genesis 2 and 3. It is an initial eschatology that is brought to the forefront, magnified, identified and located within Israel's last days framework. Now watch this.

The Old Testament law –
Paul said the resurrection would be when the law which is the strength of sin, would be removed.

But the law is the Old Testament law. We've already demonstrated that by Paul's use of the term, the Torah. Now notice, James has, at least initially, seemed to agree with that, but his answer here, really basically whichever position you want to take, whether it's the law of Genesis 2 and 3 or whether it's the Levitical system, James agrees that both of those were removed in AD70. Therefore, resurrection. **Chart 49e.**

Resurrection When Sin Put Away (1 Cor. 15:56)

But Sin Finally Put Away by End of 70 Weeks (Daniel 9:24)
End of 70 Weeks AD 70.

Therefore, Resurrection at AD 70

Let's go back to this point about sin.
Resurrection would be when sin would be put away in fulfillment of Israel's promises (Isaiah 25, Hosea 13).

But sin would be finally put away by the end of the 70 weeks. That is God's promise to Israel.

Seventy weeks are determined to put away sin.

Therefore, resurrection would be in AD70.

Let's go to chart 49g.

Resurrection When Sin Conquered

Resurrection Has Not Happened (Jordan)

Therefore, Sin Has Not Been Conquered

How Then John 8:51 / 1 John 5:13?

I want you to notice, ladies and gentlemen, resurrection would be when God would deal with sin. But according to James and all futurist eschatologies, the resurrection has not occurred. Then God has not dealt with sin. I suggest to you that is an unavoidable argument. You say, well, it's an "already, but not yet." But for Paul, the putting away of sin, when God would deal with sin so that man could live in his presence once again would be at the end of Israel's Old Covenant history.

And then James says, the physical resurrection that Israel saw and they were a part of Israel's world view. Well, number one, he didn't give us a text proving what he needed to prove.

Secondly, we have to ask the question, because of what Israel saw, they expected this. Here's the great question: *Were their expectations appropriate?* They saw Israel nationally restored in the return from Babylonian captivity. Does that mean they were justified to expect nationalistic restoration in Jesus' day? Well, they came to Jesus, tried to establish a nationalistic restoration, by putting him on a throne. But Jesus, when he perceived that they were about to come and make him king, he withdrew himself.

You see, they had seen nationalistic restoration over and over and over. That led them to believe in a future nationalistic eschatological restoration, and Jesus said, you guys are wrong, you just don't get it. It is spiritual. And I believe I'm out of time.

James Jordan's– Third Negative

Well, that last was a good argument. I'm not sure my argument really completely stands up in light of that point, because I agree that we cannot rely too heavily on what first century Jews thought.

I want to also touch on a couple of points and then do something else. Don argued that there's a problem with dichotomizing the judgment on the *oikoumene* and on Israel. That's not my intention. They're two sides of one coin. I'm saying that the history of Israel goes from being Abraham and his clan, his sheikdom, to a nation in the times of Moses, a nation that incorporates a very large number of Gentiles, mixed multitudes, after the wilderness wanderings. You know they don't do circumcision for forty years in the wilderness, and then they enter the land and they circumcise everybody, and that includes a whole lot of Gentiles. They all become Israelites there. And then the nation is changed again. It's geographical boundaries change in the days of Solomon. This nation changed again at the restoration. This *oikoumene* is tied to it.

So this is one package here. So I see that when Paul says judgment is coming upon the *oikoumene*, I think it is a technical term referring to this empire that God sets up, which is his empire, which is presided over by Gabriel, just as Israel is presided over by Michael. But that this is all part of, sort of Israel in a very large way. This is the arena that's coming under judgment. So I think the judgment there is two sides of one coin and not two different things.

The argument was made that types go from the physical and natural to the spiritual. That's 1 Corinthians 15 which has obviously come up quite a bit. This is a passage that it would take forever to argue out, so there's no point in that, but I want to look at verse 46, "the spiritual is not first, but the natural, and then the spiritual." He goes on, you're familiar with the passage.

The question is, what's the meaning of the word "spiritual" here? Does it mean immaterial, or does it mean, empowered by the Holy Spirit? Because if it means that the spiritual world order, the spiritual mode of existence – the original spiritual mode of existence in the Garden was in just exactly this kind of body and the implication seems to be -- I mean I take the passage in the conventional way, myself – that there is a different, more glorious kind of physical body that is more thoroughly permeated and energized by the Holy Spirit, and that's what's meant. It's not a matter/spirit dichotomy here implied in any kind of a way.

Along these lines, I don't wish to imply that anyone in the consistent preterist camp believes that the body or the creation is evil. I do sense a certain notion that it's inadequate for the world to come. And we agree on that. That's why those of us who hold traditional views believe that in the world to come, we're going to have a different kind of body that's capable of doing cooler kinds of things.

I believe that Adam died on the day he sinned, or would have, but that an animal was substituted for him. Animal death can kind of keep you alive for a while but eventually the judgment falls. That's why eventually the blood of bulls and goats don't take away the judgment, they don't take away the liabilities for sins, they don't cover them permanently. I think that what was supposed to have happened to Adam in connection to eating of the tree, happened. The tree was his ticket out of the Garden into the wider world. It was what he would be brought to when he was old enough and mature enough to handle mature responsibilities. He would be more like God. And all these things did come to pass: His eyes were opened. He became more like God discerning good and evil. In Genesis 1, what God does is this: He sees and pronounces things good. That's what God does.

Babies don't have the wisdom to make those judgments. Adam was supposed to learn wisdom from this serpent, who was the wisest animal, and over a course in time mature in wisdom to where he would be given the right to eat of the tree, get knowledge of good and evil, and become a king in the land. If you study the phrase, "knowledge of good and evil," it's always associated with kings. David has knowledge of good and evil. Solomon prays for knowledge of good and evil to be able to rule.

So to leave the Garden sanctuary and go out into the land – all those things happened – it could not happen except going through some type of death and resurrection experience that would actually enable him to handle the problems in the wider world. He wasn't able to do that. So whatever complex of things is there, definitely things happened that first day. I think the fullness of the judgment that could have come upon him was averted by the death of the animal that got killed in order to make covering for him, which is what the Levitical system does. So, so much, just for some quick points of clarification.

I think what I should like to do is deal with this millennium question as best I can. I have to say, the presentations that Don made, comparing scripture with scripture, are all things that I would have to look at in detail because the same language can be used for three or four kinds of events in the Bible, because there all these typological recurrences of the events that take place in the Bible. So the real question is not, is the same kind of event taking place, but is it the same event? And that would take some time. But I will share with you what I think is going on in Revelation and why I think the millennium starts in AD70. And at least that will put that out on the table, and maybe, or maybe not, we can interact on it.

As I see it in Revelation 4, Jesus is not in heaven, and there are 24 thrones and there are 24 elders on the thrones and the question is, what are these 24 elders? Because of the King James Greek text, it has been assumed for a long time by many commentators that the 24 elders represent human beings in heaven before Jesus is there. Because in the King James text, it says, "Worthy are you to take the book because you have purchased *us* from every tribe, tongue, and nation, and made *us* to be the kings and priests to our God, and we will reign on the earth."

Well, if that's the case, then there were people in heaven before Jesus was. That doesn't make any sense to me, and I don't think that's possible. I think the context in Revelation, the meaning of the book, and the teaching of the Bible as a whole, would indicate to us that these would have to be angels. And so there are plenty of other Greek texts that say, "You purchased *men* from every tribe and tongue and people and nation, and made them to be kings and priests." So they're angels praising. These are angels sitting on thrones around the throne of God. They are His assistant rulers in the Old Testament. These are archangels, there're 24 of them, they are the heavenly models for the 24 chief priests, the 24 chief Levite musicians, and the 24 chief Levite guardians of the temple. The whole set of 24 plus one high priest is here. There's the Angel of the Lord and they're 24 angelic elders who had these thrones, who ruled with Him in heaven.

Well, the lamb approaching the throne is the ascension of Jesus. The lamb begins to open up the book of the completion of covenant history. And it's been restrained. There are seven seals that have held back the coming of the kingdom. So he breaks them one at a time, and each time he breaks a seal, something is revealed that has been held back, and when he breaks the sixth seal – this is where it gets important, I think, in chapter six, verse 9 -- when he breaks the sixth seal, "I saw underneath the altar the souls of those who had been slain because of the word of God and because of the testimony that they had maintained." Note two phrases in Revelation: there're those who are slain for the word of God and the testimony of Jesus. And that refers to the New Testament martyrs. And then there are those who are slain for the word of God and for something else, for their testimony. This refers to those who have perished under the Old Covenant before Pentecost, before the Apostolic church. So where are they? They're under the altar. What altar?

My guess is they're under the incense altar which is the ladder between the firmament heavens and the highest heavens symbolically and would be an appropriate place for them. They're not in the highest heavens, they're not in the throne room of God. They're still waiting. That's not bad. This is Abraham's bosom; this is paradise. But it's not good enough. They cry out with a loud voice saying, "How long, oh Lord, Holy and True, will You restrain from judging and avenging our blood." Each one was given a white robe and they were told to rest a little while longer until the number of their fellow servants and their brethren who were to be killed even as they had been should be completed also. Now who were these? Well, they're the final harvest of Israel that we're about to see in the book.

These people, these saints from the Old Testament times, Israelites, Gentiles, whoever believed under the old age covenants, they're all waiting, waiting to get into heaven. Jesus is gone into heaven, so now why can't we? It's open now, isn't it? And they're told to wait a little bit longer cause there's one more group of people supposed to join them. Hebrews makes the same point where it says, "apart from us in this last generation, they don't receive this perfection." So continuing in the sixth seal, the world starts to come to an end. I don't believe the sixth seal is an AD70 event; I believe the sixth seal, where there's an earthquake and the sun becomes black, and the stars start to fall from the sky, is right there at the beginning but it stopped. It's like it all stops in mid-air so that one last opportunity can be given to Israel. That's the witness that will bring about the conversion of the 144,000 along with and unnumbered multitude of Gentiles. They are from the nations, tribes, peoples, and tongues. That's the phrase that designates Gentiles. These two groups are just like coming out of Egypt. These two groups are saved during this time for the final great opportunity that comes to them.

Well what happens to these people? Well, we could read all of chapter seven, but we won't. We all know that these were coming out of the great tribulation. I think it applies also to the entire period. If we go to chapter eleven, verses 7-12, we come down, I believe, to the great tribulation passages in Revelation. The witnesses are killed. Who are these witnesses? They're parallel in Revelation to the 144,000 who are going to be killed in chapter 14. They are killed in the city that is mystically Sodom and Egypt. I don't know that that actually refers to the physical city of Jerusalem. For this city I go back to Zechariah 2, where they are told that in the restoration age they will be in a Jerusalem without walls.

This Jerusalem without walls will consist of God's people spread out as the four winds throughout the *oikoumene* bearing witness for Him. Then of course you have the Babylon without walls, the mystery Babylon in Zechariah 5. I think that underlies this. So I would say that the mystical Babylon, mystical, evil Jerusalem, is simply the Jews and the Judaizers wherever they are in the empire– focused on the land, focused even more in the city in the temple, but wherever. And they persecute the witnesses, which is the symbol for the testimony of two witnesses of the church.

But then after the seven trumpets, we have what in the book of Revelation is the aftermath of the trumpets. We have thematic discussion of what's beginning to go on here and importantly becomes chapter 14. We have a transition here, an historical transition. John says in chapter 14 of Revelation, "I looked and behold a Lamb was standing on Mount Zion, and with Him one hundred and forty-four thousand, having His name, the name of His Father, written on their foreheads." Well, there they are. This is the people that were set aside and now they are on the earth. In terms of the imagery of the book, they are an earthly expression of God's kingdom, and they are described in symbolic language. They are not defiled with women, they are chaste men, they're virgins -- obviously not literal language, but important language.

Then we have these two harvests: the one on a white cloud, the son of man, puts in his sickle and reaps the earth of grain; and then an angel is told to gather the grapes, and the grapes are trodden out in the great wine press outside the city.

Now look, the harvest of bread and wine is the harvest of saints. This is not a judgment on the wicked here. And "outside the city" -- immediate reference to the book of Hebrews. Let's go outside the city and join in with suffering whatever is necessary to advance the kingdom of God. It doesn't say they were trodden under the wrath of God. Literally, it says in Greek that wrath-wine was produced. This wrath-wine is blood and it covers the whole land. Well, what does blood on the land do? It cries for vengeance, right? So, it was a lot of blood, a lot of vengeance. All these bowls.

Well, what happens in chapter 15? How do I know that these were the saints who are harvested in chapter 14? Because in 15:2, as it continues, "I saw as it were a sea of glass mixed with fire and those who had come off victorious from the beast were standing on the sea of glass holding harps for God." These are the people who were waiting under the altar and they have moved up in terms of the architecture to being on the firmament. Being right there. But they still can't go into the most holy because the temple is filled with smoke and the glory of God, and no one is able to enter the temple until the seven plagues and seven angels are finished.

Well, what's been going on in this book is there are 24 archangels up there. Each one of them has a thing to do. You want to spend a whole lot of money, you can get this [referring to a set of 204 lectures on Revelation, which at the time on cassettes sold for $1000.00 – JBJ], and I will show you where those 24 archangels are. Each one of them has this thing to do. Seven trumpet angels, seven bowl angels, four guardian angels at the Euphrates, four harvesting angels in chapter 14, and two strong angels. Each time one of those angels does his thing, he takes off his crown, puts it in front of the throne, goes out, leaves his chair empty and does his thing. At this point all the angels are out. There's nobody in this temple, the thrones are vacant. They're waiting to be occupied. This is my argument for the progression of the book. Angels have now yielded their guardianship.

By the way, to me the proof that the book of Revelation was written before AD70 is that angels are bringing judgments. I don't agree with most of Ken Gentry's arguments for the book's date. I don't think the city is a literal city. I don't think the temple that's described in chapter 11 is the temple in Jerusalem. I think it is a spiritual Temple. I don't think 666 is Nero. I think it's an anthropic number, which means it's a Jewish number. It refers to the high priest and to the Herods which are the two horns on the lamb. Gentry's are traditional kinds of proofs, and I don't think they're needed.

We know that angels supervise the old creation, angels are the ones who come and bring judgments on it. The fact that angels are bringing these judgments means that it's the end of the old creation, the one administered by angels, and the book has to have been written before that time. QED. We don't need the big books to prove that. It's real simple, see. We don't need a big fat book. We just need one page from this book [holding up my small paperback *A Brief Reader's Guide to Revelation* – JBJ]. And there you've got it. Well, at any rate....

So now you see, I think, these angels have now vacated their thrones. Men are now going to take over. Men are now come of age. In Christ, men and women will join with him ruling the world. As Paul says, "Don't you know that we're going to judge the angels?" It's all going to be reversed. We were the officers all along, but we were cadets and the sergeants were over us, but now we've graduated and we're officers over the sergeants.

So right now they're not on these thrones, they're not in heaven, they're waiting outside the door. But in chapter 20, "I saw thrones and they sat on them and judgment was given to them." As I read the book, that's just continuing the story. If this story is in sequence, then this event of occupying the thrones means the angels' thrones. I don't see what other thrones they can be. Has to be something that comes after the events of the book. That's why I think the millennium starts at this point. Saints who were departed who have been waiting in Sheol and Paradise, now take the angelic thrones and begin to rule. But then you see this is going to come to an end at some point.

The same time those who were beheaded because of the testimony of Jesus and the word of God – now these are the New Testament church martyrs. Who are they? They're all beheaded, they're all like John the Baptist, they're all Nazarites. Go back and read the law of the Nazarite. It says the Nazarite cuts off his dedicated head and puts it in the fire and sends it up as an offering to God. It doesn't say he cuts his hair. That's what he's really doing. But repeatedly, it talks about his head, his dedicated head. These are those who have been Nazarites of God, holy warriors, that includes everybody including the most humble. And they are now coming to life again and reigning with Christ for a thousand years. I think that refers to the resurrection of the church on earth, this army church.

Well, that's how I see it. And I know that there're all kinds of parallels between the end of the millennium here, but when it's over, Satan is released out of his prison to deceive the nations. Well, he's deceived the nations already in the book, but he's now been chained up so he can't deceive the nations. That doesn't mean he can't do anything in my opinion. It means he can't do *that*. There is a falling away – some kind of falling away, that is yet future. He is destroyed at this point and that's his final throne judgment.

Just a final point. Don has used the expression, an eschatology for Israel or Christian eschatology, an eschatology for the church. I don't think it's so much an eschatology for the church as it is, I think, the larger part of the original Adamic eschatology. I guess we're going to have to continue with that tomorrow. When I say that the destruction of Jerusalem in AD70 brings the entire Adamic world to an end, I mean the political structural sense, but I think more is implied than that. And I will present some arguments tomorrow. I hate to say, "already, but not yet," because that's such a slogan, and it's so empty. You've got to fill in. What's already, and what's not yet? But I think those categories are somewhat helpful and I think there's a definitive legal transition from death to life to glory that happens in the middle of history, but there's an outworking of it in history that's progressive in certain ways and reaches a climax toward the end. Of course, that's conventional eschatology, but I still think that's what's there. At any rate, that's how I view the millennium and we'll just have to decide which of us is right.

JAMES JORDAN– FIRST AFFIRMATIVE

Resolved: The Bible teaches that all human beings will be raised to new physical bodies at the end of the present Christian age.

My proposition is concerning the physical nature of the resurrection at the end of the present Christian age. You know, that looks a whole lot like that other thing we were talking about and as a matter of fact, these are all so tied together that I haven't even broken them apart in my mind or in trying to think about what I could bring here for you. And so, that's what I've been talking about right along. In fact, I talked about the physical body yesterday, and today I'll probably talk about the thing we were supposed to talk about yesterday which is more argument to the second coming in the traditional sense. But this is all the same stuff, you know.

I do want to define what I understand by physical bodies, and I spent a lot of time yesterday trying to show you the physical expectations in the Bible, the this-worldly, physical, bodily nature of reality, and that there would not have been any expectation on the part of Jews in the first century to whom the New Testament was actually written first of anything else. I don't guess I persuaded you, but that was my argument. But, it is sometimes heard that we are going to get this same body back. And, obviously, we're not going to get this same body back. In the traditional Christian view you can't be that. You know, grass grows up out of the molecules of your buried body and then it gets eaten by animals and something else eats it and all the rest. No one's ever maintained anything like that and nowadays we know enough to know that every ten years or so, you don't have the same body you had.

If a train leaves New York City going to Los Angeles and it gets to Chicago and they remove three-fourths of the cars and put on a bunch more cars, and it gets to Sante Fe, and they switch the engine and the caboose out and take all the rest of the cars that left New York City and put some more cars on and it gets to Los Angeles, is it the same train? Why yes, it's the same train, even though none of the cars are the same. It's the same train because of certain things, it travels in time. So I understand that whatever the soul is, whatever the inner part of a person is in heaven, is simply re-embodied in recognizably the same configuration, but glorified at the end.

With Jesus now, the actual molecules that were in the tomb were the molecules that were transfigured in his transfigured body when he was resurrected, but it doesn't have to be the same molecules. It has to be the same body. That's what I understand to be the Christian historical position that I was trying to get you in sympathy with in my talk yesterday and a little bit more today. Beyond that I'm not going to try to engage in a bunch of textual arguments. We could do that, but it's very long to do that. And I mostly agree with Mr. Grace, and by the way, I'm not Dr. Jordan, I'm Mr. Jordan. Well, His Holiness Jordan, but not Dr. Jordan, just don't have an earned doctorate.

I haven't found that arguing over theological matters gets you very far. You just don't get persuaded. When I was in seminary, Baptists and Paedobaptists would argue over verses, but that doesn't generally come out very far. Every now and then you strike home with an argument like that, but more it's a matter of saying, does this make sense? Does an individualistic understanding of baptism based on personal profession make sense of all the biblical data and the biblical world view, or does the idea that whole families or whole groups of people are baptized because of their certain relationships with each other make more sense? You get farther with that.

So that's really what I want to do, have been doing, and will continue to try to do here. And that's not to say there's no place for arguing text. But if we were to get into an argument about what 1 Corinthians 15 really says, you couldn't do it in two hours. I believe the word *soma* almost always means this, in the New Testament, and does not very often mean other things. It can, but it doesn't, but I'm not going to argue for that. What I'm going to argue for is that the biblical understanding of time in history leads one to believe in the final end to the history that we are presently in. And I want to do that by saying a bunch of things that you will agree with and then make an application that some of you, at least, will question.

But let's ask ourselves why the Bible is so fat. You know, we tend to think that the biblical narrative, the biblical story is about sin and salvation, but if that's all that was involved, ten pages would do it.

You know, the second child of Adam and Eve might have been the incarnation of the second person of the trinity and the death of Jesus-Abel would have paid for all the sins of the world, and that would have set the world to rights and then we would just go on from there. There's no need for 4,000 years of biblical narrating history before the son comes into the world to save us. We don't need all this. We certainly do not need all this material here if it's just about salvation and redemption.

But it's not, it's three interwoven stories in the Bible that are constantly going on. One of them is the story of salvation. One of them is the holy war, and one of them is the maturation and development of the human consciousness and of the human race. All three of these things are going on. And I want to talk about these three interwoven stories to develop something of a biblical philosophy and history with you in the little time we have.

So let's talk about what I think is the most, well, what is clearly the most fundamental story of the Bible, and that is the story of the maturation of the images of God -- growing in the likeness of God. I am of the school of thought that says the image of God is not lost, it's not defaced, it's not shrunk, it doesn't increase. The image of God is just what human beings are. Human beings in hell are images of God. That's just so by definition. The word *image of God* means human being. The word *human being* means *image of God* .

But likeness of God can be increased, can be distorted, can be shrunk down. "Behold the man has become more like us," says God. Likeness is what we mature in, what the early church called *deification*. It didn't mean that we become gods, but that we grow in God-likeness, we grow from glory to glory according to the likeness of God. What we call glorification, that's what God is about. And that's all history would have been if Satan hadn't rebelled and started the holy war, and then man hadn't sinned and started the need for salvation. We didn't start with those things, we just got a story of maturation. That's where it starts.

Now to understand that story we have to understand some geography. And I just want to give you a simple diagram of the initial geography of the world. We're told that in the beginning, God created the heavens and the earth and the earth was formless, shapeless and empty. The earth had three things, three problems in the earth. They're not bad problems, they're just undeveloped. The earth was shapeless, empty, and dark, and the spirit of God was moving over the surface of the water.

Over the next seven days, God deals with these problems – darkness on the first day, shapelessness on the second day by putting in the firmament, emptiness on the third day by putting plants all over the earth, lighting in on the fourth day (this is a chiasm; this is the fundamental chiasm in the Bible), filling again on the fifth day matching the third day, birds and fish fill the land and the sea. Then on the sixth day, forming again: the man who is under God and over the world, the one who is going to continue to form the world; and then returning to the theme of light, on the Sabbath.

This gives us a world in which there is an original heaven that is made perfect and there is an earth which is shapeless, empty, and dark. And then this world begins to grow according to the image more patterned there so that throughout history "thy will is done on earth as it is in heaven." The earth is maturing to become like heaven. The things that are there are being reproduced here gradually and the seven days of creation start this. Then we also notice that God introduces on the second day this firmament barrier between heaven and earth. That on the first day heaven and earth were face to face, but on the second day there is a veil between the two.

Now the heart of my argument is going to be that this was introduced on the second day, and it's not permanent. It has to go away. When earth has matured to the point where it's supposed to be, this veil comes down and the marriage takes place. That has not happened. It's happened at one level – at a socio-political level -- through the history of Israel and into the New Testament, but it has not happened in the physical dimension the world started off with. To me this is a good argument. Of course, it's a paradigm argument – fits within my paradigm. But I want to present that argument to you, and then you can chew on it. You can chew it up.

Now these seven events, theses seven days in Genesis One are copied in Genesis Two at a second level. Once again there's water all over the earth, and then God forms man which is the light, and then God puts in the Garden, which is equivalent to the firmament, between the high land of Eden and the rest of the world. I am going to draw that out to you. And if you've never noticed Genesis Two tracks Genesis One there is proof for that in this book here, and so, if you really want it, a lot of my book, *Creation in Six Days*, deals with this.

The chiasm structure in Genesis One points to, I think I've got it here [displaying a copy of my monograph, *The Seven-Fold Covenant Structure*, published by Geneva Ministries – JBJ], an indication of at least some of the fifty or so other places in the Bible where exactly that seven-fold chiasm is found, like the whole book of Isaiah which follows Genesis One's seven sections, and so forth. It's pretty fundamental biblical literary pattern.

Well, what about this Garden? Because this is where this process of growth and maturation is going to begin. It says in verse eight, "Yahweh God planted the Garden toward the east in Eden," or literally, eastward in Eden, "and he placed there the man whom he had formed." So, this earth down here looks like this [drawing diagram on board]. Somewhere in here there is the land of Eden, and on the east side of it there is a Garden of Eden and there are other lands out here, like Havilah and Cush. A river arose in Eden, in the land of Eden, it went through the Garden which means the Garden is lower than the land, and then it broke out to become four rivers. We can identify these. I think this is the pre-flood world equivalent of the Tigris, Euphrates, Jordan and the river of Egypt. And here's old Havilah down here and Cush.

What do we have here? Well, we have a land of Eden, which I'm going to call a throne land. Man is not there. Man is in the Garden, or sanctuary, and lower down is the rest of the world. Now this is absolutely basic biblical geography, and if you are interested, I have lots of diagrams and pictures of this as it continues through the Bible. Now this is a copy of this heavenly-veil/world phenomena, and it's reproduced again in the holy of holies, the holy place, the mountain top of the altar, and the world down here.

Now, what about this place? Man does not start in the high land of Eden. He's not in there. He's in this in-between place in the Garden. I believe we can say with little question that if Adam had been faithful, that at some point he would have been invited up into the throne land. In that he was not faithful, he was asked to leave and then forced to leave downward. So that you come up to where the cherubim are guarding this Garden. The Garden is the entrance into the land. Sanctuary is how you get into the kingdom.

Now, when might this have happened? When was it supposed to have happened? Well it was supposed to happen at the tree of knowledge of good and evil. Yesterday we talked about the fact that there is a death and resurrection in Genesis Two where Adam goes into deep-sleep and is called up out of deep-sleep into a new life glorified by having a woman who is the glory of the man. And I pointed out to you, that a lot of people haven't noticed this over the years. God says to Adam and Eve, "Every tree shall be for you to eat from," which means the tree of the knowledge of good and evil, and there's a lot of aspects of that.

For instance, how much did Eve know? Eve did not hear God say, "Don't eat of the tree of the knowledge of good and evil." What Eve heard was, "Every tree shall be food for you." So how did Eve know that she wasn't supposed eat of the knowledge of good and evil tree? Adam told her. So when the serpent comes and says, "Did God say...," well, she doesn't have any first-order knowledge of that. But she says, "Yes, God said we shouldn't eat of this tree." That's because she believes Adam, because she didn't hear God say it. These are all very important features of the story that are often overlooked.

Well, what is the knowledge of good and evil? Every now and then somebody will say to me, "Well, it says every tree that has fruit that bears seed inside of it shall be food for you, and maybe the tree of the knowledge of good and evil didn't have seed inside of it, so maybe they were never supposed to eat of the tree of the knowledge of good and evil." And I can usually show you that's not the case because the Old Testament is full of people who have knowledge of good and evil. So it's obviously been eaten of.

We're told that children don't have knowledge of good and evil. We're told in the book of Hebrews that it's for those who had their senses exercised to become mature who have knowledge of good and evil.

We find that David had knowledge of good and evil. We find that Solomon asks for knowledge of good and evil so that he can rule as a king in the land. That's probably about the most relevant part. We find in Deuteronomy the small children don't have knowledge of good and evil; that aged, senile people who no longer can really discern things very well have lost the knowledge of good and evil. Knowledge of good and evil has to do with passing judgments and particularly in the land, not in the sanctuary. And, if you want more information on that, it's in this book. See, how nice I brought all these books along, and now you have to have them all. But here in *Primeval Saints* I have discussed this theme at some length and show the various passages because people are confused about it. It's associated with kings; it's associated with land; it's associated with being more like God. And it's acquired through death and resurrection.

Adam is going to go through some type of good-death and other kinds of good-death, maybe a bit more intense than what he went through in Genesis Two where he was ripped in half and a New Covenant was made. That's how New Covenants are made – something's ripped in half and then put back together again. That's what happened to Adam. He was ripped in half, he woke up, resurrected. There's a New Covenant because there's a woman there, marriage is a covenant, and then he's put back together again because they are one flesh. See, he's torn in half and in one flesh put back together again. That's how covenants are made. The tabernacle is torn in half in the days of Eli. A hundred years later the two parts of it are put back together again in the temple as a glorified thing. Death and resurrection. Tearing apart and putting back together again. Giving new and glorified form. That's how things are proceeding in the Bible.

Well, this maturation process, then. Adam as a baby is naked in the Garden. When he eats of the knowledge of good and evil, God clothes him. What does He clothe him with? He clothes him with the tunic, that's what it says, *chiton*. Tunics are garments of authority. Priests wear tunics. Kings wear tunics. The only other tunic in Genesis is Joseph's tunic, which is the sign of his authority.

In fact the whole business of authority-robes is very important in the Joseph stories. Daddy gives him a robe. The brothers tear it off. Potiphar gives him a robe. Potiphar's wife takes it off. And Pharaoh gives him a robe, and nobody takes it off after Pharaoh gives him a robe. It's important. God says, "All right, you have eaten this fruit. You're kings. I'm going to send you out into the world. You can rule out there. I'll give you a royal robe. I'll kill an animal to give it to you so that you don't have to die right now. It can be postponed. You'll have to die eventually."

We talked about that some yesterday, but would Adam eventually have fallen asleep and made room for new people? I imagine so. Animals too. People say, "Ah well, animals would never have died if man hadn't sinned." Well, if that was true, in 20 years, the earth would have been covered with bunny rabbits. You know, you've got to move off and make room for others. I think there's an eschatology there that's apart from sin. Death as we experience it now has sting, but I don't know what would have happened actually, but maybe they would have moved out into the planets, or something, I don't know.

What was I talking about? I don't have all this written down today. This is so informal, you know, it's just so informal. All right, informality. An informal debate. I'm running out of time.

Okay, now, how is this going to happen? Well, Adam needs to grow in wisdom. He needs to have his senses exercised so that he's ready for this process of being given this more mature form of life, this kingship kind of life. Whatever it's going to involve.

It's first going to involve physical change. He was divided in half. The second probably involves physical change as well. See now, see where I'm going. Physical change. But he's going to rule the land, so God brings the wisest citizen of the land into the Garden to help teach him. The serpent, the wisest of the field animals out of the land is brought in to teach Adam how to be wise so that he can go out into the land and be in charge.

Now who is this serpent? Well, we know that behind him is a fallen angel, perhaps not yet fallen. Lucifer, the chief instructor of humanity there along with all the other angels who were instructors of humanity. Very briefly, the way to understand this is that human beings were like cadets who were destined to become lieutenants. But they're in boot camp and the angels are the sergeants. But when you're in boot camp, you salute the sergeant, and you do what the sergeant says, and you are under law. But there comes a day when you graduate, and they pin a lieutenant's bar on you and as you march out, the sergeant stands there and he salutes you. And he's very proud that you've turned out to be such a good officer. And he tells everybody, "That captain over there, he's one of the guys that I shaped up when he was a young cadet." See? That's the way it's supposed to work. But what if the sergeant says, "Hey I don't want any officers over me, I want to be in charge forever"? Well, then you understand the fall of Satan. Satan does not want human beings to ascend over him.

Man was made a little lower than the angels, but he is supposed to be crowned with glory and honor because human beings are the sons of God and the human race is the daughter of God. Daughter Zion, Daughter Jerusalem, not Daughter *of* Zion, Daughter *of* Jerusalem, that is a very confusing thing. What is the Daughter *of* Zion? There is no such thing. This is not a positive use of the construction [the Hebrew "construct state" – JBJ]. Daughter Zion, Daughter Jerusalem is to grow up to become a bride and a queen from being a baby. And we as sons are to grow up from being little boys to being kings, then, even beyond that, to being prophets. There's a whole lot in the Bible about this, and one of the reasons the Bible is so fat is that it's concerned with this.

The first part of the Bible gives us law. Law is for priests. Law tells you what to do. The priest never has to make any decisions. All he has to do is look and see if you've got a white spot on your arm or not. And then, does the flesh show through? Well if I don't understand what Paul means by flesh, a good place to start is Leviticus. Notice the flesh showing through, then he just looks in the book. Well, shut him up for seven days, check again. It's all written out. Priest never has to made any decisions. He just follows the law, and the law says do this, don't do that. It's all right and wrong.

Then you get to kingly, the second part of the Bible. You get the kingly literature. It's wisdom literature because king does not make decisions between right and wrong. King has to make wise decisions and often deal with the lesser of two evils. Just like an army commander. That's why army people become kings in the Bible, somebody who says I'm going to have to send these men to attack the enemy and to almost certain death to enable these other guys to flank around from the side and capture the enemy from behind. Well, that's not an easy decision to make. And there's no book that tells you exactly how to do it either. You have to apply the principles you learn from the law, so wisdom literature comes in here, and wisdom is for the land.

Law is for the sanctuary, wisdom is for the land, and then the third form of literature is prophecy which is the highest form of human talk. The prophet is somebody who tears down an old world and builds a new one by his words alone, by providing vision. And he says the kinds of things that people cannot forget, and causes them to walk in new paths and makes a new order of life. That's the nature of prophetic talk. The prophet is somebody who's actually a member of God's council that God consults. And the prophet is the most aged form, the most mature form. So human beings are supposed to mature in this. They are supposed to go from the Garden into the land and into the world.

Garden, sanctuary, tabernacle, that's the emphasis in the Sinaitic covenant times. The emphasis -- we have priests, but we don't yet have kings. Kings – the emphasis in on the land. Prophets – emphasis is on the world. Abraham builds altars. Jacob – out in the land. Joseph – out in the world. The first sin in the sanctuary – stealing from God, impatience – Abraham manages not to do that. The second sin, murdering the brother. Jacob manages not to get murdered. The third sin, inter-marrying with the pagans. Joseph manages not to be seduced into sexual relations with a pagan woman, but Judah does, so that's thematically there.

The first phase of Israel's history, the Sinaitic period, the sins are primarily other gods, rebellion against the Father. The second period, war between north and south, brother-brother sins, brother murders brother in the kingly households, that's the emphasis. The third period, the prophetic age – Malachi, Ezra, Nehemiah, all about inter-marriage. I have a little pamphlet out there called, *Crisis Opportunity in the Christian Future,* which discusses this and shows this theme through the Bible. This is the maturation and development aspect of things.

Now, so far, that doesn't seem to have anything to do with our topic. But I want to get back to it, but before I do I need to talk about the other two things, and how much time do I have now. Five minutes? Well then let me briefly start into the second part of the story that's in the Bible.

And that is the holy war. Now this is a very odd thing, but Protestants just don't do much with this any more. It's like we're all pacifists. I like, when I speak – speak at two pastors groups which I do occasionally – ask how many of them wore a uniform, how many of them have ever been in the military. You know, I look and, there'll be a hundred pastors in the room, and three or four of them will put their hands up. Well, the fundamental analogy in the Bible for worship is the military analogy – we are the host of the Lord of Hosts. Read the Psalms – they're all about warfare – even the peaceful Psalms like Psalm 23. It says, "You will prepare a table before me in the presence of my enemies." You are surrounded by enemies. You are in an army camp when you sing Psalm 23. The priests are dressed in armor, the high priest garment is called armor. When Ephesians 6 tells us that we dress in armor, that's taken from the armor of the high priest with some other things added in. For instance, as I said yesterday, priests don't have shoes, but we do in our armor because we're marching out into the world. This is just fundamental and we don't know much of anything about it. We have a whole vast number of clergy who have no real feel for combat, for war. You can get that by studying it without ever having been in the military. But the academic preparation divorced from any consideration of these things leads to distortion and our ability to understand the Bible. And it means that one of the major themes in the Bible gets overlooked.

You know, what is Jesus doing for most of the gospels. He's beating up demons. Why is all that in there? If he just came to save us from sin, he could just suffer and die. Instead, he's at war. And so we have in the early church what was sometimes called the *Christus Victor* teaching – Jesus is victorious over the enemy which is ultimately the angelic world, principalities and powers. But that theme doesn't get noticed very much, and we need to notice it because the holy war starts in the Garden.

The serpent starts out pretty good. He comes to Eve and says, "Hi, I'm going to help you become wise," and he says, "Was it God who said you shall not eat of any tree in the Garden? Did God say you can't eat of any of them?" "Oh, no, no, no," she says, "we can eat of any of the trees, but the tree that's in the middle of the Garden, God said, because I believe my husband, and he's my pastor, and God has mediated to me through this man – you shall not eat it and you shouldn't touch it either. We were talking about it, and Adam and I figured out that, you know, if we shouldn't eat it, we shouldn't touch it." Now everybody seems to think that this was wrong on her part. Well, if you want to know if it's wrong or right to deduce that, read Leviticus Chapter 11, and you'll find that what you don't eat, you don't touch, and so her unfallen process of reasoning is absolutely correct. They are beginning to see the implications of the command. This reasoning is right.

Then -- and I have a friend who argues that this is the instant at which Satan makes his decision and falls – the serpent says, "You will not die." Then he continues to say things that are true. "In the day you eat of it, your eyes will be opened." Well, we know that's what happened. "And you will be like God." Well, God says they'll become more like Us. And "you'll know good and evil." God says, "Yep, they've got knowledge of good and evil." Okay, so what is knowledge of good and evil again? It's the right to pass judgments. What's in Genesis One? "God saw that it was good."

God's eyes were open to pass judgments on good and evil. God said, "it's not good for the man to be alone." God's eyes see, his eyelids are open. That's the sense in which their eyes will be open. That's the sense in which they will be passing judgments on good and evil. As God said to Laban, "Don't you speak good or evil concerning Jacob." See, there again, Laban's come out with a whole bunch of men. He's going to have law court, he's going to have a trial, he's going to pass judgment, and God says, "No, you're not. Nope, you're not going to do that, Laban." This is the way the language is used from Genesis and throughout.

Well, he now is not going to be giving wisdom, this angelic tutor. No, from keeping the law, you get wisdom. From breaking the law, you get anti-wisdom. And now, that's what he's going to be bringing in.

And in fact, Satan is replaced as the angelic tutor of God's people, isn't he? That's why we have the angel of the Lord – pre-incarnate Jesus Christ. He doesn't *become* an angel, but he comes taking Satan's *role* to be the teacher of us during our childhood before he comes and actually is incarnated as a man. Well that's the beginning of the holy war.

I want to talk about that just a little bit, talk again about the tree of the knowledge of good and evil, and what its additional meaning now is that we've got to deal with Satan, and then talk about sin and redemption. And then I want to make an application of that to the eschatological question of the resurrection of the body and all that stuff. Now, it's Don's turn.

Don K. Preston's First Negative

Let me begin by saying again how much I appreciate the opportunity to be here and to be with you and engage in these discussions with James Jordan. As I stated yesterday I have appreciated his writings and his work for many years and still do. Obviously, I take issue with that, and before I get into some of the things that he said here this morning I want to cover again, or really I'd like to cover some things that he brought up yesterday that I never got to develop fully, but that I think are important for you to understand and for those that will get the tape, I think It's important to have this information out there.

I presented several charts yesterday demonstrating the direct parallel between Revelation 6, Revelation 12, Revelation 14, Revelation 16 with Revelation 20. We have the themes and the motifs of the past suffering, the victory of the saints, that is, the binding of Satan, and the threat of future more suffering, the promise of the victory of God, that is, the ultimate victory of God and the new creation. I demonstrated that in chapter 6, 12, 14 and 16 that those themes are developed within the context of the past suffering of the martyrs, and they were to be vindicated at the day of the Lord in AD70. Therefore, the question was, since we have the exact themes, motifs, and time references in chapter 20, it seemed to me that the consistency of those patterns demands that we take Revelation 20, as culminating, that is, the end of the millennium, in AD70 as well.

James' response to that was that basically we're dealing with similar language, and certainly I would agree with James in this one area, that is just because you find similar language does not demand, does not demand that you're dealing with the identical thing. There is such a thing as illegitimate totality transfer which means, okay, you take all of this evidence and you impose it on the text where it doesn't belong. I don't want to be guilty of that, and I try not to be guilty of that. However, what must be demonstrated, instead of simply saying, well that's not proper to do, it has to be proven. And the way that James approached in trying to discount those parallels, as I understood his approach, as I understood his argument, was that all these previous chapters we have Old Testament martyrs being vindicated, rightfully stated. That's the fall of Jerusalem in AD70. However, in chapter 20, we have New Testament saints, New Testament martyrs, and that comes at the time of the fall of Jerusalem.

In other words beginning at the millennium in AD70 and going onward, we anticipated a time in which New Testament martyrs would be vindicated at the so-called end of time. Well, I really believe that that overlooks the fact that there's an absolute, may I use the term, organic unity in the biblical concept of soteriology. Let's go to Matthew 23. In Matthew 23 Jesus stood in the temple and castigated Old Covenant Israel for their sin. Now I want you to notice that that sin, of course, obviously, it involves many things, but that sin involved killing the prophets. And I would like to pick up with verse 29.

"Woe to you, scribes and Pharisees, hypocrites! Because you build the tombs of the prophets and adorn the monuments of the righteous, and say, 'If we had lived in the days of the fathers, we would not have been partakers with them in the blood of the prophets.' Therefore you are witnesses against yourselves that you are sons of those who murdered the prophets. Fill up, then, the measure of your fathers' guilt. Serpents, brood of vipers! How can you escape the condemnation of hell?" or Gehenna, "Therefore, indeed, I send you prophets..."

Now, notice, here's the past suffering of the Old Covenant saints and prophets. But notice what Jesus does, "Behold I send to you..." Here are what you and I would generally speak of as New Covenant saints, New Testament saints. I send you prophets, wise men and scribes, some of them you will kill and crucify and some of them you will scourge in your synagogues and persecute from city to city." In other words, Jesus saw a, insofar as the eschatological scheme is concerned, he saw an absolute unbreakable bond between the Old Testament martyrs and those martyrs of his saints that he was about to send out. Furthermore, I would pull it out, that Paul saw – Paul is certainly a Christian, is he not -- but Paul saw himself and the apostolate as playing, the pivotal, consummate role in filling up the measure of eschatological suffering.

In 1 Corinthians 4, verses 9f, Paul said, "I reckon that God has set forth us, that is the apostles, last of all, as men condemned to die."

Were the apostles the last martyrs to be made, well patently not, but in God's eschatological scheme, they were appointed as those to fill up the measure. I know that because Paul says in Colossians 1:23, "I now rejoice in my sufferings for you, and I fill up in my flesh what is lacking in the afflictions of Christ." Now that's not talking about redemptive suffering – Paul does not have to suffer to redeem us. But it's talking about the eschatological suffering because God has cups. God has the cup of sin, God has the cup of suffering, God has the cup of wrath, well obviously God has the cup of blessing as well. Well, when the cup of sin is filled up through the persecution of the saints, the cup of suffering, God's cup of wrath is poured out. That's exactly what we see in the book of Revelation. My point being that you cannot delineate between the Old Covenant saints in Revelation 6, Revelation 12, Revelation 14, Revelation 16, and the saints in Revelation 20. Why? Well, because in Revelation 14, and specifically Revelation 18, we find that the city Babylon has killed, not just Old Covenant saints, but they have killed the apostles and prophets of Jesus Christ. These are New Testament saints, and as a result of that her cup is now full. Thus, I would argue, and I don't see personally how that could be avoided. I see that unbreakable bond between the Old Covenant and the New Covenant saints in God's scheme of redemption insofar as the eschatological suffering is concerned. I don't see a dichotomy between those sufferings in the New Testament.

Then James made an argument yesterday, in response to my argument that you simply cannot dichotomize, you cannot separate the eschatological promise to Israel, that is the resurrection of the dead, 1 Corinthians 15, Acts 24, 1 Thessalonians 4, from God's promises to Old Covenant Israel. And James said, well, there are those promises that lying behind them, as the over-arching eschatology, is Genesis 1 and 2.

Well, again, my problem with that is, that Paul ties both of those, if you want to say both eschatologies, Paul ties the Genesis 1-3 eschatology in with his eschatology related to Israel's promises in 1 Corinthians 15. In 1 Corinthians 15:22, "As in Adam all men die, even so in Christ shall all men be made alive." There's the Genesis eschatology, if you please. But when would that be fulfilled? When would that Genesis eschatology come to fruition? Well, it would be when "death shall be swallowed up in victory" which is the fulfillment of Isaiah 25:8, which is an Old Covenant promise made to Israel.

Now I would remind you that James, in response to my written question, said, "All of God's promises to Old Covenant Israel were fulfilled by AD70, and that all of the Old Covenant law, Matthew 5:17-18, was fulfilled by AD70. I would remind you that Jesus said not one jot or one tittle of the old law – now remember the law foretold the resurrection of the dead, the ultimate, eschatological end of the millennium resurrection, the law foretold that. And Jesus said not one jot nor one tittle could pass from the law until every iota of it was fulfilled. Therefore, of absolute necessity, unless the resurrection has occurred, that Old Covenant, not some of it, not a little bit of it, not most of it, but the entirety of every jot and tittle of that Old Covenant law, and that's inclusive of the animal sacrifices, remains valid today. My point again, is, that you cannot delineate between an eschatology of Genesis and an eschatology of Israel. Paul saw no further in Paul's soteriology and in Paul's eschatology, Paul saw no further than the fulfillment of God's promises to Old Covenant Israel, and that's evident in 1 Corinthians 15.

All right, insofar as some of the things that he said specifically in his affirmative now, let me get on to that, and I hope I haven't overlooked some things that I needed to that he addressed yesterday, and I hope I've completely covered those. Be that as it may, James says that he believes that it's necessary that this current world order come to an end. Now mind you his proposition affirms that all human beings will be raised in physical bodies at the end of the current Christian age. James, on the board here, gave us an awful lot of information, some of that's just pretty cool, as a matter of fact. I like some of that, I really do, and I've always enjoyed his writings in regard to development of a lot of things. But James made a statement that personally I find rather disturbing and which I find antithetical to the biblical eschatology. And James says, "I don't want to argue over verses, because that doesn't make sense." So what James is trying to do is develop a world view and then see if that fits the scriptures. That paradigm it seems to me is reversed. I would suggest to you that unless we can go to specific verses and develop our paradigm from specific verses, from the compilation even, of specific verses, that we do not have, number 1 we cannot develop a world view and number two, we most assuredly cannot have a correct paradigm. To suggest, for instance, that we should not go to 1 Corinthians 15, believe me I understand what he says when he says it would take us a long time to go through 1 Corinthians 15. Yeah, it would but you see that exegetical demonstration of the validity of his argument or mine is what really is at stake. I would suggest to you that what is at state here is not, well okay, in the Old Testament, we had this heaven and earth of Assyria that came to an end and we had the heaven and earth of Babylon that came to an end and we had the heaven and earth of Israel that came to an end in 586 BC, therefore we extrapolate from that to be in a current Christian age, I would suggest to you that that's not a valid hermeneutic. Now does it appear on the surface that that has some validity? I would even grant on the surface of it, well, that sounds good – heaven and earth ends, heaven and earth ends, heaven and earth ends, heaven and earth ends, okay, there well might be. But here's the problem with it.

When we look at the biblical concept of the ages – I want to make an assertion here. Now this is a broad, generic assertion, all right. Can I find exceptions to this assertion? Well, most assuredly I can in the Rabbinic literature. But the point of fact is, here's the fact. The Jews believed in two ages. Emile Schurer, in his work on the times of Christ, Lightfoot, just about anybody, and on and on we could go, demonstrate that the Jews believed in only two ages.

What they called this age and they weren't speaking of the Christian age, but they spoke of this age and the age to come, the *ha olam ha-bah.* That's interesting by the way, in the New Testament times they changed that and in the Greek, it is the age that is about to come. Why did they change it from simply the age to come, to the age that is about to come? Because they realized that they were living in the fullness of the age. Nonetheless, they believed in only two ages. What they called, "this age" was the age of Moses and the law, that's the age of Jerusalem and the temple. The age to come was the age of the Messiah and the New Covenant. It's the new creation, it's the age of the kingdom.

Now watch this very carefully – point number three. The Jews believed that "this age" the age of Moses and the law. Now is there a controversy about that? In some Rabbinic circles, most assuredly there is. Again I'm generalizing, and what is most important here is not necessarily what the Jews commonly believed but the question is, is this what the New Testament teaches? And the answer to that is unequivocally, "Yes." But the Jews believed that the age of Moses and the law would end, but the age of the Messiah and the New Covenant would never end. Now, please, catch the power of that. In what age was Jesus living? Jesus was living when he said, "If any man sin against the son of man, it shall be forgiven him, but if any man sin against the holy spirit it shall not be forgiven him neither in this age or the age to come. Jesus wasn't talking about some after the end of time scenario or else there will be the possibility of sinning against the holy spirit after the so-called end of time. Jesus was staying within the framework of his Jewish mentality. But I want you to notice again the key point is that the Bible asserts that the age of the Messiah, the age of the kingdom, the age of the New Covenant would never end. In Isaiah 9:6-9, speaking of the coming of the Messiah and his kingdom, it says, of the increase of his government – that's the kingdom, that's evangelism – of the increase of his government and of peace there will be no end.

Now here's my problem with James' paradigm. While I certainly agree that the heaven and earth of Assyria passed away, the heaven and earth of Babylon passed away, the heaven and earth of Egypt passed away, the heaven and earth of Israel passed away in 721, and in 586, the problem with extrapolating from that to the end of the Christian age is that it runs smack dead into a steel wall of the inspired statements of scripture that the Christian age, the age of the kingdom of the Messiah, has no end. You cannot, therefore, take the recurring themes back here and say, well, that looks like a good thing, that looks like a good paradigm, and extrapolate that into a direct contradiction about the emphatic statements about the unending nature of the kingdom in which we are in now. Because these emphatic statements are a direct contradiction of that recurring paradigm. In other words that paradigm is good up to a point. And then the paradigm stops, and it stops in the face of Daniel 2:44, Daniel 7:13, Luke 31:32-33, the God of heaven will give, as he spoke to Mary about Jesus, "shall give him the throne of his father David, and of his kingdom and of his throne, there will be no end." Well, how can you speak about the end of the current Christian age, the end of the current reign of Jesus Christ, if the Bible affirms in unequivocal terms that it has no end.

And in Ephesians 3:20-21, of course, "Unto him that is God, be glory in the church by Jesus Christ throughout all ages, throughout all generations, age without end." As F. F. Bruce said in his commentary on Ephesians, "That is the strongest Greek term for endlessness, that the Greeks possessed."

Let me go on, I've got to hurry here. Next Chart. (Chart number unknown) Here's the argument: The kingdom that is the church age has no end. The disciples in Matthew 24:3, and James is arguing for, now the disciples, I'm suggesting, did not ask about the end of the current Christian age; they asked about the end of the age represented by the temple. Now, did that temple actually represent the Christian age? Did that Old Covenant temple represent Christ and his New Covenant age? No, it did not, and you know it did not.

That Old Covenant temple represented the law of Moses, it represented, "this age," their "this age," and it was supposed to give way to the *ha olam ha-ba*, the age to come, the everlasting age of the Messiah. When did that Old Covenant temple which represented "this age" pass away? We know the answer to that, it was in AD 70.

All right. The disciples asked about the end of the age. But the church age has no end. Therefore, the end of the age, about which they were asking and the discussion that we are having today, cannot refer to the end of the current Christian age. I would suggest to you as kindly as possible that that within itself mitigates James' proposition.

Let's go on very quickly. James says the Bible is not just about salvation history, but is about several things. He admits of course naturally, that it is about salvation history, but it is also about the maturation of man and the image of God. Boy, I'd like to spend three or four lessons on the image of God. I agree with Ward Fenley that the image of God has been restored in Jesus Christ. I will simply give some references, and I've been preaching over the last several Sundays on the image of God if you'd like to have a copy of those tapes, you can contact me, and I'll be glad to provide those. But I would like to take notice of the fact that Paul's theology was that the image of God was being recreated in the first century in the body of Christ, the church, Colossians 3, Ephesians, 4; even Peter gets in on the act in 2 Peter 1, when he says according to his divine power, he has given us all things that pertain unto life and godliness through the knowledge of our Lord and Savior Jesus Christ. And it was through that knowledge, he said, that we are becoming partakers of the divine image, or the divine nature. For Peter and for Paul, that image of God was being re-created in man at that time. Certainly, I agree with James, they were not becoming God, but the image of God was be created in them. And so Paul, as he anticipated, the eschatological resurrection says, as we have borne the image of the earthy, we shall also bear the image of, and I thought man was already in the image of God, the heavenly. No it was lost in Adam. But Paul anticipating resurrection which would come at the end of the fulfillment, the consummation of God's promises to Israel was still anticipating bearing, taking once again the image of God.

Now James said, when the earth matures, the veil is taken away. Well, let's look at several situations on this. Turn with me, please, to Ephesians 1. I would even agree with that to a great extent in principle, let me say. But when we look at what the Bible has to say about when the veil between God and man, that separation, was to be removed, the Bible is very emphatic about it.

In Ephesians 1, in that great longest sentence in the New Testament, starting with Ephesians 1:3f. I only have time for verse 10. But notice in verse nine, he says, that, "it was God's eternal purpose which he purposed in himself to do what? That in the dispensation, that in the stewardship of the fullness of time, he might gather together in one all things in Christ, both which are in heaven and which are on earth in him. What was God's purpose? God's purpose in Christ was to reunite heaven and earth. We saw a lesson yesterday about Genesis 28, about the ladder from heaven to earth, men and angels ascending and descending on it. What is that? The barrier is gone. Heaven and earth are re-united. This was to be done in the fullness of time. Well, what is the fullness of time? Is it the end of the Christian age? Not according to Paul. In Galatians 4:4, in the fullness of time God sent forth his son, born of a woman, made under the law. I know when the fullness of time was. It was the Old Covenant age, the end of the Old Covenant age. What is the theme of Ephesians? It is the story of God bringing man and heaven back together even as he anticipates in 3:14, "For this reason, I bow my knees unto God the Father of our Lord Jesus Christ from whom the whole family in heaven and earth is named." You see the time of the removing of the barrier had come because of Christ's work on the cross to be consummated by the parousia. The time of taking the barrier away had arrived.

Well, let's go on and examine that in Hebrews 9. (Chart 64a). James said, and I agree with him, that Genesis 2, in the barrier, is recreated in the temple with the Most Holy Place and the holy place. Well, you have the veil, then the Most Holy Place. What's on that veil? Picture of heaven and earth, isn't it? That's what Josephus says is on the veil. And that veil represented the separation and the alienation between God, between heaven and earth. Josephus calls the Most Holy Place, heaven, and he calls the holy place, earth, in Antiquities, book 3. So what are we doing here?

Now, I want to make an argument here, and I want you to follow along with this. This is somewhat technical, it's based upon the Greek text, but I'll try to make this as simple as I can because it deals with this barrier concept. And it deals with when this barrier, this veil, if you please, of the temple, the veil of Genesis 2, as James would express it.

Now watch. Israel's eschatological hope, the time of reformation of Hebrews 9:10, when access to the Most Holy Place would be made available. Well, when would access to the Most Holy Place be made available? When the veil was gone. The holy spirit indicating this that the way into the most holy is not yet made manifest while that first tabernacle still has standing, still has validity. No access to God, the veil is there, as long as the Old Covenant stood. OK, that veil is the constant reminder of this but the time of reformation, you see, that Old Covenant would stand until, that barrier would stand, until the time of reformation. Greek word, *diorthosis*.

OK, now watch this. But the *diorthosis* is a really cool Old Testament word for the time in which God was going to restore Israel and restore Jerusalem at the coming of the Lord in the judgment of all men and the time of the reward, Isaiah 62:7f. I don't have time to develop that because time is getting away. Be glad to develop that further.

But Israel's *diorthosis* would come, Isaiah 62, at the fulfillment of Israel's prophetic corpus. Israel's *diorthosis*, the fulfillment of the typological prophetic cultus of the Old Covenant high priest and the day or worship, day of atonement, would be fulfilled, when? When the high priestly function was fulfilled, and it would be fulfilled at the time of reformation.

Now watch this, Israel's *diorthosis* would be realized at the end, that is the time of the fulfillment of Israel's old testament ceremonial cultus including the high priests daily, or atonement service, on the day of atonement. Therefore, the coming of the Lord for salvation which is Hebrews 9:28, which is the time when? When that veil would be removed and man could come into the Most Holy Place. That veil, that separation, would be removed at the time of the second eschatological coming of Christ at the end of the millennium. When would that take place? At the time of the fulfilment of the day of atonement cultic symbolism of the Old Covenant. Therefore, the coming of the Lord for salvation, Mt. 16:27, Hebrews 9:28, would occur when the prophetic actions of Israel's ceremonial cultus, including the sacrifices and the high priest actions, were fulfilled, in other words at the end of the Old Testament cultus. Next chart.

Now, I want you to see what we have in Jesus Christ. What we have prior to Christ is all these recurring themes, the symbolism, the typology, happening over and over, but Christ is no longer the shadow, Christ is the body, he is the fulfillment. Now watch this. Just as the high priest offered the sacrifice, Jesus appeared to put away sin by the sacrifice of himself, Hebrews 9:26. Just as the high priest entered the Most Holy Place with the blood, Jesus entered the Most Holy Place there to prepare it, Hebrews 9:24. And just as the high priest had to come out of the Most Holy Place to consummate the atonement, Jesus had to return to complete the atonement, to consummate that atonement process. And the writer of Hebrews says, still within that discussion of that complex of Christ's redemptive work, says, "in a very, very little while," hosan, hosan micron is the Greek. In a very, very little while, the one who is coming, will come and will not tarry.

So here we have the promise of the ultimate eschatological, end of the millennium, second coming of Christ to bring salvation in fulfillment of the Old Covenant types and shadows, to bring that world of types and shadows to an end, to bring salvation to its completion. But, again, when would that occur? Those things were imposed, that is, the Old Covenant, was imposed until the time of reformation. If Christ has not come in fulfillment of every single aspect of those practices, of that cultus, then that cultus still stands valid today.

Let's go on. Let me shift gears right here. James says, if you want to see what Paul means by *flesh*, go back and see the book of Leviticus. Well, I would really challenge that because Paul says in Romans, 8, in one of his longest discussions of *flesh* found anywhere in his writings, "You are not in the flesh, but in the spirit." Paul wasn't talking about this, was he? He wasn't talking to disembodied spirits, but he was talking to people who were no longer living a certain type of life. He says, you are not in the flesh, and he says, if you are in the flesh, well if we go back to Leviticus for a definition of flesh, we're in trouble in Romans 8. No, we have to see how Paul is using flesh, and I would challenge the concept that when Paul, in most of his eschatological discussions, all of his eschatological discussions, as a matter of fact, uses soma, I would challenge the assertion that he is talking about this, (Preston indicated the physical body) as well. So I think that's a very debatable issue.

Very quickly, he brought up the issue of the holy war. Now I happen to agree with James on this point. I think the Bible is about the holy war. But where do we see the consummation of that? We see the consummation, the beginning of conflict in Jesus in his ministry, we see it at the cross, where Jesus triumphed over principalities and powers, we see that in 2 Corinthians 10, where Paul says, "The weapons of our warfare are not carnal." But we see the culmination of that conflict, the ultimate victory, in Revelation 16 and Revelation 20, but Revelation 16, that final victory is when? When God's wrath is completed in the pouring out of wrath under the 7th vial in the city of Babylon which is where the Lord was slain. It's Old Covenant Jerusalem. Therefore, while I certainly agree with the holy war concept, the holy war is consummated in AD 70 with the destruction of Jerusalem, and the wedding then takes place. The spirit and the bride say, "Come. All things are ready." Thank you.

James Jordan's Second Affirmative

There was so much in that last talk that I must refute, I won't be able to get back to my own presentation! (wink!) Actually, I should like to clarify a couple of things. I think that the ascension of saints in Revelation 20 is inclusive of the apostolic age saints. I'm sorry I wasn't clear about that, but I believe the saints of the Old Covenant history are awaiting their ascension and then they are joined in chapter 14 by the martyrs of the apostolic age and then all ascend together in AD70. But see, I think that starts the millennium. But I'm not dividing those up into two groups. What about people after that? Well, chapter 14 says, "Blessed are the dead who die in the Lord from now on." In other words, now you don't have to go to paradise or Abraham's bosom or sheol, or whatever you want to call it. We don't know very much about this place, but you don't go there and have to wait. Now you go straight in. At any rate, I don't think we disagree on that particular point there.

Now, Don's argument, part of it, from 1 Corinthians 15, and I'm not trying to say that we can't discuss exegesis; I'm trying to say that I think we have somewhat... I'm trying to lay a context in which my exegesis will be shown to be obviously correct. But as I understand it, one of the arguments that Don gave, is that 1 Corinthians 15 says that death is swallowed up in victory. And this comes from Isaiah 25, verse 8, which has to do with Israel's future, and therefore, 1 Corinthians 15 has to do with Israel's future. Now, my problem with that, is that, if we look at Isaiah 25, we find that it indeed says this, God is going to do these great things in the future.

Chapter 26 continues, "In that day this song will be sung in the land of Judah;" chapter 27 continues, "In that day the Lord will punish Leviathan, the serpent;" and 27:12, says, "In that day the Lord will start his threshing from the flowing stream of the Euphrates;" and then verse 13 says, "It will come about also in that day that a great trumpet will be blown and those who were perishing in the land of Assyria and who were scattered in the land of Egypt will come and worship Yahweh in the holy mountain of Jerusalem."

In short, "death is swallowed up in victory" was fulfilled by Cyrus at the end of the exile. In a sense, you see. And this is where it becomes complicated to me. Obviously, that's not the fullness of the fulfillment any more than when Jeremiah says, "the New Covenant will be made, not like the one with the fathers, and in that very same time Jerusalem will be rebuilt," and other language that has to do with the return from exile – that's not the fullness of it. But there are these multiple stages of fulfillment. So yes, in Isaiah, it's in Israel's future, but that doesn't prove that when it's quoted in 1 Corinthians, it necessarily is. Might be, but it doesn't do it. This could be applied in more senses. There's a sense in which that going into exile is death, going into Assyria is death.

Jonah inside that fish is in deep-sleep and talks about being dead. He says he's in sheol. Well, I hope I don't have to argue with you that Jonah's being inside the fish and then being put back out, is teaching him that going into Assyria is to be protected in the midst of the sea, and then coming back out again is the return from Assyria. That death and resurrection happens to Israel when they go into exile. They're in death; they're in sheol just as Jonah is in sheol, under the earth, inside the fish, and then they come out again. So death is swallowed up in victory? Yes. Cyrus! And the book of Isaiah has a great deal of stuff about Cyrus. And why? Why is Cyrus on board? Well, it's easy for us to see. He's a type of Jesus. But notice the stuff starts there. So that's the kind of question we need to bear in mind. We can't necessarily jump from one place to the other. At least, that's my argument.

Now Don said that the present age in which we are in will never come to an end. That we are in the final age, and I completely agree. Don just didn't need to prove that because I would have granted it right off the bat. But, you see, that doesn't mean that this age doesn't have ages within it, and in fact, Ephesians says in 2:7: "In order that in the ages to come, he might show the surpassing riches of his grace in kindness toward us in Christ Jesus."

We read in the scriptures the phrase, "the age of ages." So what that says to me is that the new age which began at Pentecost, there is an age within that, which I would say was 40 years, a new wilderness time, until AD 70. I believe there's another period within that final age which we're in right now, and I believe that there is another period within that final age which comes after what the church has traditionally talked about as the second coming, the final coming of

Jesus Christ. And that the change in the physical world is just the last application of what has already started. Yes, in the most important sense, this age will never end because the new age that begins at Pentecost in a definitive way is the final age. There is no more foundational work that can be laid. Jesus has done it all, but the applications of that obviously are going on and on in history. And so, what does the Bible indicate about how that going on and on is going to be?

I should like to say this as well. I don't know if Don will buy this or not. There is a variety of consistent preterists or neo-preterists, or whatever your term is. I'm just not going to let you call yourselves preterist because I'm a preterist. We need consistent, full, whatever. I won't say hyper-preterist, except to say that I won't say it. I'll be nice; I used to be meaner about this than I am. I don't use the word heresy anymore. I apologize for using it in the past. Please forgive me if you were ever offended by that. I really do think this is a serious error, to be honest with you, but I don't like, I've grown up beyond using that kind of rhetoric because it's not easily understood, and it's offensive, so I don't want to be offensive, okay?

But, you see, I think that for most of us – I don't know where Don would fall out on this -- the new age begins at Pentecost and the old age ends at cataclysm, a New Testament word that I have picked up for AD 70 out of Matthew 24's cataclysm, the new flood. That's the end of the old. Some of this is overlapping time when Paul writes Ishmael and Isaac are both in the house and so forth. New stuff comes at Pentecost. But you see, here again, if we start looking at it, the new age begins in its full way in connection with the resurrection, ascension, Pentecost, and Jesus, then it starts to flow out and the implications of it. No further implications come to pass. Extra stuff that Jesus needs to finish up bringing us down to AD 70, and beyond that the age goes on.

But as I have argued with you, and I could give you lots of kinds of arguments for it that the New Covenant begins with Cyrus in very important ways. All that stuff in Zechariah about a 49-fold lampstand, this huge outpouring, Ezekiel's temple, all that cool stuff is New Covenant, new creation stuff. The gospel already: we have Gentiles under the government of God in a way that they weren't. That actually begins to be anticipated with the Remnant covenant which is made at the center of the book of Kings. The Davidic covenant comes at the center of the book of Samuel. The Remnant covenant in the center of the book of Kings is made through Elijah who is taken back out to Mt. Sinai, and God passes in front of him like he did with Moses and gives him the new rules. And one of them is, "you go and anoint Hazael king of Syria." That is really radically new.

God is extending his kingdom claim over another nation. It's not going to be a seed-nation, but already, you see this is a new thing that's kind of starting up. This extension of the kingdom directly over these other nations. So there are beginnings that come before the beginning. And if the beginning is really sharply defined at Pentecost, yet it also begins in Jesus' miracles and it continues to begin on down to AD70. The old age ends in AD 70.

I think in the religious construct sense, everything from Adam. We are no longer under the sky in the same way. Remember in Genesis, chapter one, it says, the sun, moon, the lights were put in the sky for signs and for seasons. The word seasons there doesn't mean fall, winter, spring. The word means festival occasions, *mo`ed*, like in the word *har-magedd-on*, the mountain of festival assembly, the feast of tabernacles where this battle takes place in Revelation.

How do you know when to worship God? Well you see the sky starting to become bright before the sun comes up, that's when you offer a morning sacrifice. The sun goes down, as soon as it's down, before it's completely dark, you offer the evening sacrifice. The sun tells you when to worship, and the sun and the moon together tell you when to come to feasts. You watch for the vernal equinox, you watch for the first new moon after that, count fourteen days, and it's Passover. The sun and the moon tell you when to worship God.

Of course, that's not true for us any more. And that entire system, the angelic world is brought to an end in AD 70 and we're in new creation. Now my argument is going to be that in another sense, those stars still are there. In another sense that veil still is there. And what is implied is that the outworking of the separations isn't complete until you can see heaven again. But you see, when does the old age end, practically speaking, in terms of outworking? Well, it didn't end for the Igbos in South Nigeria in the year 70. It ended for them when the missionaries got there. Up until that time, their magic worked from time to time. Missionaries are universal in giving this kind of report. Unless they're all insane, missionaries can tell you that until the gospel comes, the chief of the tribe could go out into the jungle and he could talk to his stone and the stone would move or indicate to him certain answers. Not all the time, but these things went on, and there continued to be an angelic superintendence over these people. They continued to live by distorted forms of the Old Covenant, archaic, or elementary principles rules.

In the Bible you have the true form of the elementary principles, you have the true form of food laws, the true form of sex laws, the true form of taboos of time and space. All those things in their true form are in Leviticus and in the Old Covenant. That's the true form of archaic religion.

But archaic religion continues in the world until the gospel comes, and when the gospel comes it's shattered. I remember a missionary telling me that the chief came to him and said, "You know, you came here and you started peaching this, and you said the kingdom of God had arrived," and he says, "now I go into the woods, and I talk to the stone, and the stone does not move for me." And that's universal testimony of missionaries as well. You read Chinua Achebe's novel, *Things Fall Apart*, and he talks about this. But when the missionaries come, all of a sudden the old religion doesn't work, and that's what Revelation shows. There's this process whereby the gospel comes as a white horse bringing the baptismal good news, and then what follows after that is war, mother against daughter, all the things that Jesus talks about. He's not talking about political war, he's talking about those kinds of things. Then what follows is the starving out of the old stuff, as the bread becomes expensive, but a protection of the new, as the oil and the wine are protected. And then follows a green horse, which green is Levitical -- emerald is the Levitical stone that brings forth judgment. That happened in forty years. It happens again and again.

So as the gospel spreads out into the world, the things that happened to remove the old archaic order and bring in the new, the maturity, is continuing to happen as the gospel spreads over the earth. So yes, the old age ends once and for all, definitively, fully in AD 70, but as it's applied it's ongoing until at some point it's ended everywhere on the surface of the earth, and there aren't any more tribes or people groups that haven't had the old way shattered. As soon as it's shattered, you get a New Covenant.

It happened in Israel. You want to see what happened? There are no Jews any more. Their religion is around the Mishna. This is a new religion. Judaism, Mishna, Talmudic Judaism is not old testament religion. They formed a New Covenant. They had to come up with a new religion that did not involve animal sacrifices any more. They had to rework it. They get a New Covenant. It's just a counterfeit. Wherever the gospel goes, you get people who come into the church, and you get others -- they can't continue, the old ways don't work. So they have to come up with something else. They become Communists, they become different kinds of things, that's what happened all over the so-called third world. After the missionaries went there and shattered the old, some became Christians, some became something else, but they could never continue where they were.

Now that's why I think we need to have that perspective. This beginning begins, and then it really begins and then continues to kind of begin a little bit, too. The old age ends, it starts to end, it really ends in AD 70, but it continues to end in its applications. That's part of the perspective that I'm trying to bring to this.

A couple of other things. On the image of God. It's going to be a matter of how we define these terms and how we use them. Yes, Paul talks about how we are being renewed in the image of God. I'm not sure the Greek word there carries all the same aspects of the Hebrew word in the original. That's not something I want to debate. Because I think that's all a matter of: what do you mean by this, what do we think this means, does this word always mean the same thing in every context? I'll leave it at that. I haven't studied that out in years. I just formed my opinion early on and shared with you. But I'm not going to die for it. There are other things I'll die for, but not that.

Also, when I said, if you want to understand what Paul means by flesh, go to Leviticus. What I meant was that flesh in Leviticus has to do with the middle part of man where death is lodged. It doesn't mean just physical stuff. It has to do with death. When the flesh is exposed, you're dead. When stuff flows out of your flesh, it carries death. Different for us: out of our innermost parts flow rivers of living water, as the Holy Spirit proceeds from me to you and from you to me.

Back then, "back in them days," the flesh is dead, and what the flesh gives forth is death. And that conceptually, I think is laid out in Leviticus. It's never said, you see. As I said, you have to live with these symbols, you have to travel in them. And then you begin to realize, hmmm, okay, flesh, that's where death is lodged in some important way, and my skin is protecting death from having all the influence it might. There're a lot of things there. But I think that when Paul starts to talk about flesh, he writes as a Jew, and he's having those general conceptions in mind, and I don't think that we are actually in disagreement here. Maybe that's not how you'll put it, but I wasn't saying flesh where Paul means *soma*. *Soma* is more connected with physical body than the word flesh is. Richard Gaffin says the word flesh means the old way, the old dead world, and spirit indicates the new living, and life-giving world. And I think he's basically on the right page there.

And finally, in terms of comments on comments, the veil that is removed in the New Covenant in the first century is the veil that has cherubim on it. It's there between the Most Holy Place and the holy place. That's taken down. It's torn down at the cross and the book of Hebrews talks about its removal. See, that is the veil that is put up in Genesis 3, of cherubim blocking the way into the tree of life, blocking the way into the Garden, which is an image of this other one up here [pointing to the sky] that separates heaven and earth in a visible physical way. But I don't think there is any implication about the physical veil or curtain being removed then. Again, I think that we are in an age of ages, an age in which this one fundamental, final work is seeing the implications of it being worked out. One implication of it is that being in Christ means that eventually I'll have a body like he has a body. Now Don wrote to me he believes Jesus gave up his physical body in AD 70. Is that fair? That is essential? I don't accept that. So maybe you can justify, maybe you can show why you think that. It might be something we can debate about a little bit.

How much more time have I got? About ten minutes.

Let me talk a little bit more about this conception of the world that I was starting on – talk a little bit more about the holy war. Remember the first part I was talking about was the maturation. Adam is supposed to guard the Garden and to beautify the Garden. How is he going to beautify the Garden? Well, he needs something to show him how to beautify the Garden, so God makes him a babe who is an image of beauty and glory, cause the woman is the glory of the man, and the woman has beauty and she has nice long hair, and we don't get to have it. We have to be ugly. The woman is the inspiration of the man. She shows him what beauty is and that's true historically. I mean all your great literature and art – most of it's made by men inspired by women or men going out to kill dragons in order to impress girls. I mean, that's how it works. Beautifying the world is something that when men do it, they do it in order to impress women, so that part of it is taken care of.

God brings animals to Adam so that he can learn that he needs something to help him beautify the world. He's also supposed to guard the world. So God brings an animal to Adam so that Adam can learn something about guarding the world. Lucifer comes in then to challenge him. It's okay for him to challenge him. Adam may say, "You're giving me some arguments here, Snake." And Satan doesn't have to be fallen in order to play what we would call devil's advocate and teach Adam something about the need to guard the holiness of God. Fact is, Satan decides to rebel and perform that task with full intention. He really does become an enemy. And so Adam needs something to help him guard the Garden, and what he needs, he will acquire at the tree of knowledge of good and evil. That, then, becomes the second thing that the knowledge of good and evil tree will give him, not just maturity, but a weapon that will enable him to purge the Garden of the serpent. I'll come back to that in a second.

The other thing I wanted to say is, if Adam is supposed to take dominion over the Garden, dress it and keep it, he can do that. But he's also told, he and Eve together, "Be fruitful and multiply and take dominion over the entire earth." So he's going to need descendants in order to fulfill that. There're going to have to be new people coming from him, and that's an important part of the history. There's Adam, there's his descendants who move out from the Garden, and out from

Eden, downstream following the rivers out to the four corners of the earth. Now what about the holy war? Well, not just dominion, but the holy war is going to have to be fought. Not only in the Garden, but in the world. Because the serpent comes from the world. He's not native to the Garden. He's a beast of the field. And so, if he has fallen, he's bringing these fallen influences into the Garden and he's got to be purged out of that, but he's got all these fallen influences out in the world as well. And if Adam and Eve are going to take dominion over all the world, then their descendants, as they move out and take dominion over all the world, they're going to have to deal with Satan and his boys, who are usurping the world as well as the Garden. Children are needed to purge the field, the world outside the Garden.

We can only imagine what things might have been like if Adam hadn't sinned but the holy war continued on. The devil starts talking to Eve and he starts trying to seduce her to sin. She says the serpent confused me and I ate. And Paul says, that's exactly right, Eve was confused, she was led astray. Hers is a sin of inadvertency. Adam, however, was not confused. Adam heard God say, don't eat this stuff. He sinned with full knowledge, and that's why it's Adam's sin that brings the human race into sin. What Adam was supposed to do -- and we know that he was standing there the whole time, the text says so -- he was supposed to interrupt the serpent and defend his wife. She's in the Garden, he's supposed to guard the Garden, he's supposed to guard her. That's what Jesus does for us. Adam should have interposed, and said, "Honey, let's go over here and eat of this tree of life; forget this tree of knowledge," and try to get the snake away.

But we can only imagine that these attacks might have continued and gotten worse and worse, and at some point, in order to protect his bride from the devil, Adam has to die. That is, he has to experience the promised good-death connected with the tree of the knowledge of good and evil that will make him a king and give him the power to deal with the devil. That's where this goes. We have to imagine history without the holy war, just general maturation. Now we have to imagine history with the holy war, but without sin. Adam still has to fight the holy war. He's got to get Satan out of the Garden, and he and his descendants will have to go from there and get him out of the world. And then someday he will be gone from the world, and maybe you can see where I'm going with this, or where I want to go with it.

The weapon that he will need is connected with the knowledge of good and evil – kingship. Noah is the first person to be given that. Noah is given the right to exercise capital punishment. Noah is made a king. And then we have the whole history of this development of maturation and kingly power. We can't say all the details of how it would go, because the world didn't actually go that way, but to some extent we can. What do we see in history? We see enemy men, and we see demonic forces behind him, sometimes, as in Job. The raiders come into Job. Here Job is. He's a god-fearing Gentile, he's a descendant of Esau. He's king. He says, "I'm king of this land." And that's why the book is kingly wisdom literature. It's about a national disaster. What happens to Job and all these people who are dead, is a national crisis, and that's why his three friends come to him.

The word "friend" is a technical term that means advisor throughout the Bible. And these are his three cabinet members and they come to talk to him. And then the Jewish priest, Elihu, "My God is Yahweh." Yahweh is the Jewish name for God. He also is there to be consulted. He's the court prophet from Israel at this Gentile court. Well, I don't know why I'm talking about that, except to say, we see in Job that fallen angels are behind the human attackers that are going on here.

So this is the holy war that is going on and it comes out in the open in Jesus' day, and about all I'm going to be able to say here is that it's real important in the Old Testament. I mentioned earlier some of the things. Even the sacrifices in Leviticus do not have to do just with taking away sin. In fact only the Sin and Trespass offerings do. Trespass and Purification are sin offerings. Sin or Purification offering takes care of inadvertent sins, the sins of Eve, the sins of being led astray. The Trespass offering deals with high-handed sins, sins like Adam's. This is laying aside every weight, every weight, so that you can fight. You go from there to what we call the whole burnt offering but literally is Ascension offering. You ascend up to get power and then you bring the bread and wine, which is called Tribute in Leviticus 2, and those are the spoils of holy war. And finally you come to the Peace offering which is the peace that ensues after the victory in the war. All of this has to do with this holy war motif, not just taking away sin but fighting the war. Well, we return to this when I come up here again.

Don K. Preston's Second Negative

Let me begin by picking up on some concepts and ideas that James has presented. James has returned to the concept of the maturation of man. I would like for you to turn with me to Ephesians 4. There's no question whatsoever that James is right – that the Biblical theme – there is contained within the Biblical theme-- the concept of the maturation of man. It is, as a matter of fact, the eschatological goal.

But it is also posited within a specific frame work at a specific time. And there are themes and concepts associated with it, that I think are so delimiting, that is, restricting, that we cannot take them beyond our present day, that we must, in fact, contain them within the first century.

I've already called attention to the fact that, for Paul, God's scheme, God's plan, God's eternal plan–this is not contingency A or plan B – but God's ultimate goal, was to bring all things together, both of which are in heaven and which are on earth in the fullness of time. We've already identified the fullness of time.

The fullness of time is not the end of the Christian age. It was the end of the Old Covenant age. That was to be the time for the consummation of the bringing together all things. That was to be the time of the breaking down of the veil, if you please, of Genesis two, the veil of the temple.

So while James seems ostensibly to agree with me to a certain extent, and I agree with him to a certain extent, I believe that the Bible is definitive of placing the consummation, not just the beginning of the outworking of the consummation. But I believe that the Bible is definitive of pointing out for us that with the appearing of Jesus Christ, and with his parousia at the fall of Jerusalem in AD 70, to bring the Old Covenant world, in which that veil stood – that veil which represented the veil of Genesis two -- with the removal of that Old Covenant system, access into the Most Holy Place.

After all, let's look at it like this: Is not entrance into the presence of God what eschatology is all about? Being in God's presence redeemed saints, being in his presence – yeah, that's the scheme of redemption.

And by the way, I'll get to it momentarily, but I absolutely cannot agree more with what James had to say on Revelation 14:13, but we'll get there momentarily.

In Ephesians 4 Paul discusses the work of Christ. And he says, "When he ascended up on high he led captivity captive and gave gifts unto men. And he gave some to be apostles, some to be prophets, some evangelists who are teachers." To do what? I want you to notice something. For, that is, God miraculously endowed the prophets and the apostles and those early evangelists, pastors who were teachers. He miraculously (endowed) them "for the equipping of the saints for the work of the ministry, for the edifying of the body of Christ until we all come to the unity of the faith. To the measure of the stature of faith,"

I'm quoting King James and reading from the New King James, you'll have to excuse me. "Till we all come to the unity of the faith, to the knowledge of the son of man to a perfect man," *teleos*, to the mature, "perfect man, to the measure of the stature," please notice now, "of the <u>fullness</u> of Christ." Notice the concepts and the terms. "To the <u>perfect</u> man." There's the mature man. It's not the <u>beginning</u> of the maturity of the man. You see they had already started creating the man. You have put off the <u>old</u> man and put on the <u>new</u>. What were they supposed to do? Go on unto perfection, to be created fully into the image of God. Colossians 3, Ephesians4, 2 Peter 1, and what have you. But Paul says those miraculous gifts of the Holy Spirit had been given to equip the church until the arrival of the full man.

Now I asked James in a series of written questions to him before the debate, if he believed that those *charismata*, the gift of tongues, as they were manifested on Pentecost, those healings, those raisings from the dead, were still present today, and he said, "No." Well, I agree with that. I do not believe that we have the *charismata* today. Do I believe that God is with us today? Yes, I do. But, you see, to believe that God is with us, and to believe that God answers prayer, is not necessarily to imply, nor to demand, that God is with us by means of the *charismata* as it was manifested in the first century.

The key point I want you to see here is that Paul is focused on the arrival of the perfect man. Now when would that be? It would be at the time of the arrival of the "unity of the faith." I want to suggest to you, and I develop this, by the way, in my Book, *Who Is this Babylon*, that the "unity of the faith" is the full arrival, the full consummation of the mystery of God – Jew and Gentile equality in one body in Christ.

Now somebody might say, well look around, the world is still disparate, it's still this, it's still that, we have people here and people there that aren't one. That's not Paul's point.

Paul's point is not that we will ultimately arrive at the "end of the time" and everybody's going to believe the same thing. Paul was talking about an objective work of Jesus Christ to break down the barriers. Once the barriers have been broken down, the proclamation of that could then begin. And man has the choice. You and I have that choice to come into that body and to participate of the oneness which Christ has created sovereignly. We're invited into that oneness, and that oneness exists in the body of Christ, sometimes whether we like it or not.

There's a oneness there because Christ has broken down those barriers, okay? When would that mystery, when would that mature man which was the eschatological hope of Paul, when would that arrive? Well Paul said it was his personal ministry. I would call your attention to Colossians one where Paul has this to say about his personal ministry, the passage I cited earlier: "I now rejoice in my sufferings for you and fill up in my flesh what is lacking in the afflictions of Christ for the sake of his body which is the church, of which I became a minister according to the stewardship from God," now notice, "which was given to me to fulfill the word of God, the mystery, which in other ages was hidden but is now then revealed."

What is the mystery? Ephesians 3:3f, is Jew and Gentile equality in Christ. And Paul in this passage, verses 25-26 uses the emphatic mode in the Greek which Loose and Dunn and a host of other Greek scholars tell us that means Paul is saying, "I, Paul, have been distinctively chosen to bring the mystery of God to its completion." But wait a minute, the mystery of God is the "unity of *the* faith." The "unity of *the* faith" is the point of *the* maturity. The point of **the** maturity is the eschatological goal of bringing heaven and earth back together. And Paul said it was his distinctive personal ministry to complete the mystery. That means the eschatological goal is related to the first century and not beyond that. I really think that is absolutely critical.

Now I'm moving on to that. And by the way, let me very quickly state, I believe that, if that maturity of which Paul's focus was on, eschatologically has not arrived, we must have *charismata*. Because Paul said the *charismata* was given to bring that perfect man in. So if the perfect man has not arrived, there ought to be the *charismata* around. All right, let's go on.

Well James, in commenting on the martyrs, and what have you, and I hope, James, that I didn't misrepresent you in what I had to say about the Old Testament and consummation there. But he did say that those of the Old Testament joined with those in chapter 14. Well, I agree with that. I just don't think that chapter 20 starts all over. You see. I don't think it starts with a brand new set of martyrs. I think it's a recapitulation of the previous chapters that have gone before and the charts that I have put up here shows the excellent perfect harmony between these earlier chapters -- past suffering, victory and victory enthronement, etc., etc., crowns and all that kind of stuff, more suffering coming, ultimate defeat of Satan at the day of the Lord.

By the way, he did make a comment yesterday that he did not believe that Revelation six, was AD 70. I had said that he did in his earlier writings, he had said that. So I appreciate that clarification. But I would certainly disagree.

Revelation 6:12f is the Day of the Lord of AD 70. How do I know that? Because it's a direct quote from Isaiah 2:10-12 and 19-21, which Jesus in Luke 23:28-31 quotes specifically and applies to the fall of Jerusalem. Now if Jesus applies Isaiah two – which John is quoting in Revelation six – if Jesus applies Isaiah two to AD 70, what right do you and I have to apply it to something else? So I would certainly differ with his assessment of that.

Now let's go to 1 Corinthians 15 and his comments in regard to 1 Corinthians 15. I have insisted and do insist that Biblical eschatology, properly understood, is the eschatology of Old Covenant Israel. That the eschatology of the Bible is not about the end of the current Christian age as James' proposition affirms, and as all futurist eschatologies affirm in one way or the other. But I affirm and have that Biblical eschatology is related to the fulfillment of God's promises to Old Covenant Israel. I'm going to be going back to that if I have time here momentarily.

And James says, well what the problem is, you see, we have to go back to Isaiah, and we have to develop Isaiah. And I'm more than happy to do that, by the way, so let's go back there and spend just a little bit of time. I want to do this because he says that this was fulfilled in the time of Cyrus, death was swallowed up by Cyrus in the return from exile, but that is not the fullness of it. Well I agree with that. I don't have a problem saying that it is typological, I have no problem whatsoever with that.

My question is and my emphasis is, was Paul in 1 Corinthians 15 saying, I want to just take that language, I want to appropriate that language that was typological, and I want to use it in a way in which it had no original significance whatsoever, and I'm going to apply it in a totally different inappropriate way? Is that what Paul was saying? No, I don't think so; I think Paul wants us to understand that those things of the Old Covenant, and by the way, the Jews believed that all the things that happened in their Old Covenant history, were going to be recapitulated in a new way, in a magnified way in the last days.

Now are the Jews always right about everything? No, they weren't. We've seen that in these discussions. But the point of fact is, Paul does tell us that the things that happened under the Old Covenant were typological; they were signatory in their nature, but they foreshadowed and anticipated an ultimate reality. I've already pointed out in virtually every work on the typology that I'm aware of, Bullinger and others, certainly tell us that types go from physical realities to spiritual realities, from lesser significance to greater significance. I'm anxious to read Davis' work, by the way, James.

Now, the great question is, since Paul in 1 Corinthians 15, in anticipating the ultimate eschatological resurrection said, "Then shall be brought to pass the saying." Was Paul saying, well, now I know that didn't have anything in the world to do with physical resurrection, but I'm applying it that way? That's almost what we have to do, you see. I would suggest to you, however, that Paul is very much in focus with what this entire context in Isaiah 24-29 is saying (It is sometimes called the little apocalypse of the Old Covenant, and rightly so).

Let's go to Isaiah 24 and begin to take a look at the context and see what kind of death is there: "Behold the lord," Isaiah 24:1. I may have to take all the rest of my time in order to develop this properly, but I think it's important for us to see the context of Paul's discussion of death and resurrection. Paul's discussion of death and resurrection is taken from the Garden, number one. But it's also taken from the Old Covenant as he clearly says.

All right. Isaiah 24:1, "Behold the Lord makes the earth empty and makes it waste distorts its surface, and scatters abroad its inhabitants, and it shall be as with the people, so with the priest, as with the servant, so with his master; as with the maid, so with her mistress."

Let's skip down – notice verse 4: "The earth mourns and fades" – by the way, we have destruction of both heaven and earth here, don't we? That's eschatological. "The earth mourns and fades away, the world languishes and fades away, the haughty people of the earth languish, the earth is defiled under its inhabitants because they have transgressed the laws, changed the ordinance, and broken the everlasting covenant. Therefore **the** curse has devoured the earth."

Now folks, here are people who are under the curse, and it's the curse of death. But why? It is because, and by the way, this heaven and earth, whatever this heaven and earth he's talking about, this heaven and earth would be destroyed because the inhabitants had broken the everlasting covenant. Is he saying that physical heaven and earth will ultimately be destroyed because man will violate the New Covenant? No, God promised in Genesis 8 after he looked at the desolation of the universal flood and said, "I will never again destroy every living creature as I've done."

Now, we've got a choice here. Did God mean, man, that flood was messy, next time I won't be as messy, I'll just do it by fire? Was God concerned with *methodology* or was God concerned with *mercy*? The God that I know seems to be more concerned with mercy.

Thus, Genesis 8:21 is an unequivocal statement by God, rainbow in the sky and all, of saying he would never again bring a universal destruction on the earth. Well, all futurist views posit a yet future destruction, or at least re-creation, that is even greater in magnitude. Why? Well because all the air breathing animals were destroyed back there. All the fish in the sea seemingly will be destroyed this time around.

But you see, the point here is that the death that is under consideration is a sin death. It's the death of the Old Covenant. It's the death that Paul said, "I had not known sin except the law had said thou shalt not covet. I was alive once without the law; the commandment came; sin revived; and I died." Now here is a living, breathing human being saying that I died as a result of the violation of the covenant. So the death of Isaiah 24 is covenantal death, alienation and separation from God and leading to the destruction of that Old World. The destruction of the time of the judgment, verse 10, of "the city of confusion." Well, hopefully I shouldn't have to tell good Bible students what the city of confusion is.

Well in direct context of that, what did God say in the last part of Isaiah 24? "It shall come to pass in that day that the Lord will punish on high the host of the exalted ones and on the earth the kings of the earth. They will be gathered together as prisoners are gathered in the pit and shall be shut up in the prison."

Now notice, "The sun [moon] will be disgraced, and the sun ashamed; for the Lord of hosts will reign on Mount Zion and in Jerusalem." Catch this, catch this now. At the time of the destruction of heaven and earth God would rule in Zion. Well where's Zion? Well, it's supposedly on earth, right? How could you rule in Zion if earth's been destroyed? Because you've got a heavenly Zion. Now watch. God would rule in Zion and when God ruled in Zion, what would God do? Verse six of chapter 25, "And in this mountain," what mountain? Mount Zion. "The Lord of hosts will make for all people a feast," there's the Messianic banquet, folks. I don't have time to develop that, but it's a beautiful picture. "A feast of wines on the lees, of fat things full of marrow, of well-refined wines on the lees. He will destroy on this mountain the surface of the covering cast over all people." Go back to chapter 24, and see the covering, see the curse, see the death. "And he will swallow up death," what death? Chapter 24.

Now go to chapter 27 very quickly. Because the discussion of the curse, the discussion of the death, continues in chapter 26, and by the way, in chapter 26, this time of the coming of the Lord would be when the earth would disclose its blood. God would come out of heaven, walk in the mountain, and judge Israel for shedding all that innocent blood. When would Jesus Christ come to avenge the shed blood on the earth? Matthew 23.

Well, all right, chapter 27. Verse seven, "Has he struck Israel?" You see, he struck Israel because they violated the everlasting covenant. He killed them, not physically. Has he struck Israel as he struck those who struck him? Has he, Israel, been slain? Hosea 13:1. When Israel was humble before God, she was exalted. When Israel sinned with Baal, she died – covenantal death.

Yes, he has slain her, verse eight, "in measure, by sending it," or her, away: "You contended with it. He removes it by His rough wind."

Now, notice again verse 13, the passage that James brought up. "So, it shall be in that day," and by the way, this is also the day of redemption, verses 10 and 11, but the day of redemption would be when the altar, the altar at Jerusalem would be made like chalkstone.

Verse 13 – "So it shall be in that day: The great trumpet will be blown; They will come, who are about to perish in the land of Assyria, And they who are outcasts in the land of Egypt, And shall worship," – there's the sounding of the trumpet to gather together the elect of Matthew 24:31. Matthew 24:31 is the sounding of the great trumpet to gather together the dead – the dead of Israel who violated the everlasting covenant and God would offer them redemption through the Messiah. When did Jesus say that would happen? Well, verse 34 – "this generation shall not pass until all these things are fulfilled." Now my point is this – that Isaiah 24-29 do not say anything about physical death.

Jesus and the New Testament writers quote repeatedly from Isaiah 24-29. to speak of their hope of the coming eschatological consummation, the resurrection at the end of the millennium. And they say that fulfillment would be the fulfillment of Israel's promises. They never tell us it would be the fulfillment of, or a typological fulfillment. They never tell us that they are offering the nature of the identity of the death under consideration. They tell us that they are anticipating and foretelling the fulfillment of those texts and the deliverance from the death of those texts.

Well if the death of those texts is covenantal, sin death, not biological demise, then we must conclude that Paul really is talking about covenantal life and covenantal resurrection, life in the Messiah, relational resurrection, not biological resuscitation. And thus, the nature of the death, and go back to the Garden, God said, in the day you eat, you shall surely die; he didn't say, you'll start to die. He didn't say, here I'm going to kill an animal instead. Were they not cast out of the Garden that day? Were they not cast out of the presence of God that day? They died a sin death that day.

Well, I'd like to take more time on that, but, again, my point is that this eschatological hope of Paul, in 1 Corinthians 15 is based upon nothing but the promises that God made to Israel in these Old Testament passages.

Paul is not perverting. He's not allegorizing. He's not distorting, nor is he spiritualizing. Nor, I might say, is he literalizing spiritual fulfillments that were back then. Paul is not saying, well, you know there was a kind of a metaphorical resurrection that took place back there under Cyrus, but I'm telling you now, the future resurrection is going to be a physical, biological resuscitation. Paul's not telling us that. Paul says what was predicted is about to be fulfilled. Now, it seems to me we must accept that, those statements by Paul, and deal with the nature of that. Because after all, Paul's doctrine, let me re-emphasize over and over and over again, let me go back to my proposition and re-emphasize this affirmation – that the promise of the resurrection, we've spent time on it, but to me really this is the core, right here is the foundation. The promise of the resurrection was made to Old Covenant Israel; it was not made to the church. But, the promise, when Paul was speaking to the church, what was he doing?

Paul said: "I'm speaking nothing but what Moses and all the prophets said." Paul wasn't giving brand new revelation that was unknown in the prophets.

Was he clarifying and explaining? Oh yeah, no doubt about it. But it was not new revelation to the church divorced from Israel, and that's so critical to understand. Paul said that his doctrine of the resurrection as found in Romans 8, "waiting for the adoption, the redemption of our body," was made to Israel according to the flesh.

Now mind you, he didn't say it would be a fleshly resurrection. He said the promise, however, belonged to Israel after the flesh, and he's reiterating it, writing to Christians, but saying, this promise that I'm talking to you about was given to and belonged to Old Covenant Israel.

By the way, one of the reasons Paul has to do that is because some at Rome were saying, "Oh, God's already through with Israel after the flesh." And Paul asked, rhetorically, and then he answers the question, "Has God cast off His people whom he foreknew? God forbid." Absolutely not.

You see Israel's eschaton had not already arrived. Israel's eschaton is resurrection, and Paul has to address that situation, not only in Rome, but in 2 Thessalonians 2, "Don't let anyone convince you the day of the Lord has already come." He has to address it in 2 Timothy 2, Hymenaeus and Philetus are saying that the resurrection has already past. To say that the resurrection has past is to say that Israel's eschaton had come and gone. Paul says that's not true. Paul could say one of two things: Israel's eschaton has not come and gone, Romans 11, or Paul could say the resurrection has not yet come, 2 Timothy 2.

They are both saying the identical thing because Paul in Acts 26 unequivocally said, in speaking of his doctrine of the resurrection, "I stand and am judged this day for the hope of the promise that God made to our fathers..." Not a distorted change or altered promise -- "I stand and am judged this day for the hope of the promise that God made to our fathers. To this promise, our twelve tribes..." He didn't say God's through with Israel and the church is now looking for the resurrection. He said, "Our twelve tribes earnestly serving God night and day, hope to attain... Why should it be thought strange by you, Agrippa, that God raises the dead?"

Thus, let me reiterate. We cannot say well, Genesis has an eschatology, and then Paul has an eschatology. Paul's eschatology is the eschatology of Genesis carried through Israel, defined in Israel and to be consummated at the last days of Israel. As he says in 1 Corinthians 15, and of course, James and I obviously agree that 1 Corinthians 15 is the eschatological, final resurrection, but it would be the fulfillment of Israel's hope, not at the culmination of the Christian age.

Now, James says, and I fully agree, that this current age will not really end, Ephesians 2. But he says, "The new age has ages within and then there's another age at the end," if I took that down correctly. Well, I want you to notice. I believe that James' paradigm does posit, in fact, his proposition says "the end of the current Christian age." And James' view is that there's an end of time – space-time continuum as we know it now, and then there is a realm in which there is no sin. But, wait a minute.

Jesus said, "Heaven and earth," and I believe he's talking about the temple, that he's predicting the downfall of that temple that was called heaven and earth by the Jews. "Heaven and earth shall pass away, but my word ..." What is Jesus' word? Is it not the gospel to be proclaimed, to show forth the wisdom of God (Ephesians 2:7)? And is it not to convert men? Jesus said my gospel will never pass away.

Well if there comes a time in which there is no sin, no temptation, no evil, will there ever be a time in which there is no need for the preaching of the gospel? The preaching of the gospel is for the salvation of the souls of men. Jesus said, "My word," that's his word in which the proclamation of the gospel is taken to the lost will never end. Therefore to suggest a paradigm in which there's no more sin, no more temptation, no more evil, and thus the need for the proclamation of the gospel is to be contrary to what Jesus said.

Furthermore, in James' paradigm in all futurist paradigms, there is a radical disjunction between the present form of the body of Christ and the future form in that paradigm. Now I want you to take a look at

Hebrews 12, and return with me very, very quickly to Isaiah. Isaiah said that in the day of salvation in which God would destroy death, he would rule in Zion. What does the writer of Hebrews 12:21f say? He says, "You have come to Mount Zion." Folks, that is most emphatic way of say, 'You've come to the time of the resurrection promised in Isaiah 25. You've come to Mount Zion.

Well, I don't think I'm going to have time to go into Hebrews 12. But again, Hebrews 12 says, "wherefore we've received a kingdom which can never be moved. The Old Covenant kingdom was radically, eschatologically transformed. James says one day the church will be radically, eschatologically transformed. But the point of Hebrews 12 is that the kingdom that they were then receiving would never be moved, i.e., it will never be radically, eschatologically transformed. That one was, this one will not be. And I think I'm out of time.

... translate that, and then it adds, he gave gifts to men, and then the gifts are identified in verse 11 as apostles, prophets, evangelists, pastors, and teachers. Even if the apostles and prophets are gone and maybe even evangelists, no one's going to question that we still have pastors and teachers. Then what they are doing, building up to maturity and unity, it seems to me may reach a certain fullness by AD70. I don't deny that, that is the weaving together of Jew and Gentile into one new man. It's done by then. But I don't think that's the end of it. I think that's just the model that continues on.

Also, I just wanted to say the issue of typology comes up, and you know, there're all kinds of different ways to give expression to it. But certainly, one way that I would give expression to it is that we move from shadow to substance, from shadow to body. Shadows are a whole lot less material than bodies and substance are. If I'm going to trade on what is being said there it looks as if what we move from is something that is relatively insubstantial to something that is far more substantial, and that's the basic conception involved.

Now that doesn't prove anything, it's just that if we're going to try to quickly characterize typology, it's a bit more complex than what you or I believe it is, and I believe this could be substantiated, but I am not going to take time to do it. It's that Israel is a type of the world. That is the reason that there is typology connected with Israel and Israel's history is that Israel's history is a type of world history. It is a preliminary form. Israel is the priestly representation of the human race, and so what happens in connection with Israel at the center of the world is a model or what is also to be the case out here.

However, at the center of the world are all kinds of symbolic aspects that reveal things in the rest of the world but are not identical to them in terms of the specifics. If Israel's history as a model history and as a type of history it comes to an end in AD70, which it does I am firmly convinced, yet the world goes on. Is Israel's eschaton the world's eschaton? Yes, in a sense I think it is. I think that what happens to Israel in AD70 eventually will happen to the world as a whole. That's why from a conventional preterist standpoint, such as I hold, a lot of the same language is used for AD70 events and for final judgment events.

So what does the future transformation of the world look like? It looks like what happened in AD70. It's a further application of it. There's a certain definitive character to the AD70 event because it ends the entire typical history that is started with circumcision. Circumcision cut the human race in half. To be cut in half always has something to do with death. And now you've got those who are circumcised and those who aren't. They're not together. They need to come back together again. See, however, that there's a long history before that. There's a long history which still needs to have its own eschatology. So after this resurrection that comes when Jew and Gentile are joined together, there's still the rest of this. However you do that, I think you have to try to do it. So that's just another way of getting at my argument.

Don said maybe this is just a rhetorical flourish, but I'll just take it up and take it literal. He said, what is eschatology? I obviously didn't write this down perfectly, what is eschatology except the full redemption, fullness of redemption presence of God. The veil is down and has to go with eschatology to bring about our presence with God again and get us back into the Garden so-to-speak. Is that fair, Don? Okay, fair enough. That's what I'm disputing. So that makes it nice because you see I will say to you that I think the fundamental eschatology was given before man fell into sin, before there was any problem with being in the presence of God and it's this: "be fruitful and multiply and fill the earth and subdue it rule over fish in the sea and over birds in the sky and over every living thing that moves on the earth."

That is the original eschatology. It's sidetracked, it's warped, it's changed by sin. Two other things are added to it. The first thing that is added to it is the holy war because now we have to deal with these fallen angels who have sinned against God. The second thing that's added to it is the need for redemption from our own sin, and God accomplishes those things. God accomplishes redemption so that we can fight the holy war, and we fight the holy war so that we can do what we were supposed to do in the first place and that is to develop the world.

Now how is that laid out? In Genesis 1, as I said before. The instant God creates the world, the Spirit is in the world, and the Spirit is the glorifier, and he starts to glorify the world from one day to the next. Each new day ends with a step back in the evening; then the next day, a new day, a more glorious day. And the Spirit does this for six days and then, on the sixth day, the Spirit goes into a pile of dust, and now from that point on the Spirit is working through human beings to continue to glorify the world.

Human beings are the agents of transformation. What you do as images of God is the same stuff that God does in Genesis 1. You take hold of things and you divide them. You give new names to things. You distribute things out. These actions that God does in Genesis 1 are what you do. You take iron ore out of the earth; you make it hot; you separate it between dross and iron. You have separated something, just like what God does. And then you make something out of it. You give it a new name. It's not iron ore anymore, it's iron and dross, giving a new name to the things that have been divided apart. You make something out of it, you distribute it to other people. They either like or they don't like it.

I have written on this a lot and I'm quickly summarizing here. If you want more to think about that, how our actions are copies of God's actions, I can point you to more information on that. If you think about it a little you'll see that you're always doing these things. You take clothes out of the closet and put them on yourself, thus you've done an act of separation and re-decoration. You're doing the things that God does because the Spirit now is working through men to bring this world to its fulfillment.

Now to me, if man's original eschatology was to take dominion, and by implication to bring the world to perfection, then on the analogy of Genesis 1 just as God finishes his work and comes to a Sabbath, there will be a time when the human race has finished its work. Not redemptive work, but dominion-over-the-earth work.

If man is the image of God, if man's life copies God's life, then when God finished his work, the Spirit finished his work in the world, and God stopped and finished his rest, so now man, with the Spirit inside, is going to do the same kinds of things. He's going to extend this and it's going to extend down through generations, not seven days now but they're going to be fruitful and multiply. It's going to take a long time. How long we don't know, but man as the image of God will also come to his Sabbath.

I don't see a way to get around that. Well, I imagine they're ways we can always get around. That's why I'll never change my views and you'll never change yours. (*wink*) That was supposed to be humorous. Still to me that's a strong argument. Within that eschatology, the holy war eschatology and the redemption eschatology are put and they have the same shape. They go down through generations of people, and they involve things being torn in half and put back together again. The stuff that God does in the creative world, then that becomes the same kinds of things that happen to bring about holy war victories and redemption, so that you can find all kinds of parallels. This is the package of information I want in my mind as I look at, say, 1 Corinthians 15 to ask, is this talking about the end of redemption, is it talking about the holy war? It's talking about the end of the original creation. The Sabbath that's implied when man has finished his worth. Or is it all three at once, or what? Well, I'm not even answering that question. I'm saying I want all those arrows in my quiver as I assault the question.

So, that was actually part of my lecture, but I'm taking it up from what Don said. And one other thing. Yes, Revelation 6 is AD70 in a sense. But I think it starts in AD30, and then it stops. And it stops so that the 144,000 can be sealed, the last harvest of Israel, and the first fruits of the church can come to pass. Using my imagination, the stars start to fall, and they arrive near but stop, and when the bowls start, they finish falling.

So, yes the fullness of what starts there is in AD 70, is in the destruction of Jerusalem. In Revelation what is being said is Jesus has entered into heaven. From Acts we see about six months and then they stoned Steven, and that it would have been the end right there, except Steven asked that it be postponed. That's my guess.

You see, Jerusalem was not destroyed because they put Jesus to death. Jerusalem is destroyed because they put Jesus' girlfriend to death. You attack my betrothed, you know, then I'm going to kill you. The attack on the bride is what brings about the destruction of Jerusalem. Drunk on the blood of the saints, so soon as they stoned Steven, I think, by implication that's when the stars fall, but then they're given 40 years. That's how I think of it anyway.

Well, I'm going to wrap this up real quick because I think I've made my point. I mean I think my points are fairly obvious. We've got three kinds of eschatologies here, and according to the full preterist position, there is never a time when redemption is fully worked out. It's definitively worked out in Jesus, the first order application of his worked out by AD70 in the context of the Israel *oikoumene* setting, but then it continues out but it never stops. Righteousness never does really cover the earth.

As in an age of ages we can think about this age of ages. We have the age down to AD70, we have the present time of the church when the gospel has not yet gone everywhere, but we're pretty close to that. At some point the gospel will have gone everywhere and leavening work of the Holy Spirit will start to really work in the world. That'll be another phase of time, and as I've said I think there's another final phase. As I said, the present age of the church comes to an end, so within the ongoing, permanent age called the age of ages, the present age within the church will come to an end. That was my thesis and that's the way I would argue it.

I think that this is the problem. I know that Don sought to anticipate my charge by saying Jesus' word never ends and that's the word of the gospel to sinners. But see, I think that's a little bit of special pleading. I'm not at all convinced that when Jesus says, my word will stand forever, that means a word to sinners. There's lots of other kinds of words and I've tried to say that.

Then a second problem is that in the full preterist position the holy war is never completely won in the world. It's won in heaven which is where it starts. Jesus cleanses heaven. He casts out Satan and his army at his ascension. And one could argue, I guess you could make a case that the battle against principalities and powers is over by AD70 and we no longer battle against the principalities and powers. I don't know if that would be a position that some within the full preterist camp might argue: "Well, as a matter of fact, Satan is gone, period." I think that would be empirically difficult to defend, but even so, human beings are still enemies of God. Holy war as well as redemption is going on and for this position, it's never finished. But God's original purposes for the earth, that it be covered over with righteousness and fully developed, can't ever happen because there's always sin and there's always a holy war going on. God is never going to fulfill his original intention. I don't accept that. I don't see how that's acceptable.

And then finally, according to this position, the veil, the original and first veil, not typological veils, but the original and first veil between heaven and earth, is never going to come down; it's still there because you can't see into heaven, and all of that is associated in the Bible with the marriage between the created bride and the only begotten Son. So even though there are typological forms of marriage that take place, as we read in the New Testament about the marriage, the marriage is certainly taking place in AD70, no doubt about it. But it had already taken place at Mt. Sinai. Ezekiel tells us, God married Israel at Mt. Sinai. This is another iteration of it, but the fact is that the veil is there and the veil is very important.

Rebecca drops the veil between her and Isaac when they come together and then it's removed. This is symbolic action. Why do this? She puts it down, he takes it up when they marry. It implies a whole bunch of things. But, this is marital stuff. This firmament between heaven and earth is called a veil. Then if the fullness of marriage takes place, and I'm certainly not arguing for some type of physical marriage here, but I am arguing for a physical transformation. I don't think that the present world is destroyed. God says he'll never destroy the world again. 2 Peter talking about melting the elements is an AD70 event, it's an elementary thing, but I believe the world is to be transformed.

We shall all be changed is the kind of language I would use for the transformation of the universe. And I don't know how different it will actually look from the way things are now. I believe there will come a time when God's original command to Adam and his descendants is fulfilled and they have fully taken dominion over the earth. That will have happened and it will be at that point a world in which the holy war has been won. Satan has been driven not only from heaven, and not only from this or that nation, but now totally. The world is now one in which righteousness completely reigns.

So, I hope that I have at least caused you to think about some things and maybe think in some new lines of thought. Way too many details in all these positions to argue a whole lot for specifics, but what I've tried to do is give you a paradigm, some paradigms of thought that maybe will jog you a little bit so you say okay, let's think about this and let's think about what we want to do with these things. That concludes my presentation, and thank you for your courtesy.

Don K. Preston's Final Negative

Let me take just a moment here to express again my appreciation and my being honored by being invited here to be with you. I've enjoyed this very thoroughly. As Sam has said, this is a very low key and very informal discussion and it's been a lot of fun and very, very enjoyable for me and hopefully those of you who are here have benefitted from it and those who will get the tapes and listen to it in the time to come will benefit from the tapes as well.

James mentioned a debate that he saw between Gary DeMar and someone, and somebody got up and brought up a ton of stuff that hadn't been brought up. That's not fair, and I'm not going to do that either, James. But I do want to go back over some of the ground that has been covered, some of the stuff to reiterate what I have said and to re-emphasize some things that have been said and hopefully bring this to an amicable and profitable type of conclusion.

James has brought up a couple of different times about Satan being destroyed and I just very quickly want to notice the promise, the original promise of eschatology back here in Genesis. Crushing Satan's head was, in Paul's view, about to be fulfilled in Romans 16:20: "The God of peace will crush Satan under your feet shortly."

Now here's the original eschatology being quoted by Paul, saying it was about to be fulfilled very quickly, *en tachei* is the Greek. It's only used about seven times in the New Testament and it always means something very, very near. That crushing of Satan I suggest to you is the same crushing of Revelation 20.

Then moving on, to Ephesians 4, James says he does not see that as the charismatic gifts here. Well, I certainly do disagree with that. I think if you put 1 Corinthians 13 along side of Ephesians 4, you have an absolute, direct parallel. And if in fact, those are parallel, I think that can be demonstrated very, very clearly, and the question of whether or not there are actually evangelists today, I don't even really believe is the question. I believe those are charismatically endowed offices that Paul is discussing.

You know you can have somebody that is an apostle that was not an apostle of Jesus Christ, for instance. See Acts 14:14. Barnabas was an apostle, but he was not an apostle of Jesus Christ, and so you can have individuals that could be this or they could be that, but that doesn't mean that they were charismatically endowed. The question in Ephesians 4, is here is God giving gifts to men to especially equip the church to bring the church to its perfection, to its maturity, to its eschatological goal. So I would affirm since Paul specifically says that he had been entrusted with the gospel to bring the word of God, i.e. the mystery, to its consummation, Colossians 2:24-27, then since that mature man is the eschatological goal that we must honor the time frame that is Paul's generation at that particular point.

Then he makes the statement, James made the statement, I want to make sure that I get this right. Israel is a type of the world and of world history. What happens in history and in Israel, happens in the world. Well, I'm not convinced that's absolutely right in all of its senses. Take, for instance, Albert Edersheim in his book, *The Temple and Its Ministry In the Times of Jesus the Messiah.*

What Edersheim does say is that the Jews believed that on every day of atonement the world was judged. Why? Because Israel was being judged. Was Israel being typologically or symbolically, if you please, being judged that day? Well yeah, in a sense, they were. Does that mean that the entire world was present that day? Well, symbolically they were, representatively the world was being judged. Well, let me suggest to you, that in AD70 the world was representatively judged that day, representatively destroyed. That doesn't mean the world, the literal creation, has to be destroyed, because Israel was the representation of man.

I like what James has to say, Israel was a type of Adam. The problem was she was in sin. Along comes Christ to solve the problem, and that's removed *in* Christ. And so, to say that what happens in Israel happens in the world does not mean that that has to happen objectively; it means that it could and actually, historically, and theologically it did happen representatively.

And so he reiterated: what happens to Israel in AD70 will happen to the world, and thus AD70 was typological. Well, again, I really believe that's misguided. And look at Jesus' words in Matthew 24:21. Jesus, in speaking in the days leading up to the actual fall of Jerusalem, speaking of the time of the Abomination of the Desolation, and I think Josephus helps us identify that, I believe that James believes that it was the period of the Zealots and the destruction of the temple. Is the killing of the priests, right in that complex not the Abomination? To be sure, but nonetheless, Jesus said at that time there would be great tribulation such as had not been since the foundation of the world, nor ever yet shall be. Now Jesus was saying, this is consummative, this is ultimate.

Furthermore, to return to this concept, in this motif that the fulfillment or that the eschatological resurrection is the fulfillment of Israel's prophetic cult, of Israel's destiny, is not to suggest that there is another eschatology beyond that.

Now I want to address James' concept about three eschatologies here momentarily. I'll do my very best to get to that. The time is running out very quickly, but here's my point. 1 Corinthians 15, I do not believe, and Paul does not say, that it has anything to do with the restoration of material creation. Paul is speaking about dealing with the law, that is, the strength of sin and with that which is the sting of death which you said.

Folks, that's the covenantal problem. Paul is not talking about men going out and cutting down trees or building buildings and subduing animals. Paul is discussing the removal of those things that stood between man and God. Paul's ultimate eschatology, therefore, in 1 Corinthians 15 was not man subduing physical creation. Paul's ultimate eschatology, what he calls the "time of the end" (1 Corinthians 15:23f) the time of the resurrection of the dead, was the time in which the mortal would put on immortality and the corruptible would put on incorruptibility. Paul never looked beyond that, and that would be the fulfillment of the promises made to Israel. Paul did not see it as one of three, he did not see it as one of two, nor did Paul see it as one of three.

I would say in response to James' question, do all three of his proposed eschatologies happen at the same time? Well, let me answer that from my paradigm, most assuredly so. If I were to grant that there were three eschatologies, I would say that most definitively from 1 Corinthians 15, Romans 8, 1 Thessalonians, Revelation and all other eschatological passages, that the definitive eschatology was about to take place in the first century. However you would like to even discuss that or to define that ultimate eschatology, Paul and the New Testament writers never placed it far off. For them the consummation, the time of the end, the time of the resurrection, the time of redemption was always invariably placed within an imminent near context.

James says, "I would dispute that eschatology is about the reconciliation of man exclusively; it is about the earth and men on earth subduing the earth." And he says if the original eschatology was to have to have dominion, then the time will come in which man's work and dominion will be perfected just like God's work was perfected on the seventh day. And within that eschatology is the redemptive eschatology. I hope I got all that down correctly.

Well, again, let me suggest to you, that's not Paul's idea. Paul doesn't have an eschatology here, an eschatology there, an eschatology here. Paul's eschatology in 1 Corinthians 15 is the ultimate eschatology. Let me reiterate – I hope this doesn't sound too repetitive or too redundant of what I've done, but it's so fundamentally important to the entire issue of eschatology. Paul's ultimate eschatology was Israel's eschatology, the fulfillment of those prophecies made back there in Hosea, made in Isaiah, made in Ezekiel, made in Daniel, Paul never looked beyond the fulfillment of Israel's promises.

But let me reiterate, those promises made to Israel contained within them the nugget of eschatology, the core, the seed, if you please, of the eschatology of Genesis 1-3. There's no question about that. But you see, that promise of Genesis 1-3, if you want to use the terminology of original eschatology, is identified under Israel's period of time and posited at the end of Israel's time.

I see no justification, I see no evidence really, for taking the promises of eschatology beyond the promises made to Israel. Because I don't see that the New Testament writers ever looked beyond the promises made to Israel as they discuss the ultimate eschatology.

So again to address the question, James asked, is all eschatology fulfilled at one time? Yes, I believe it was. Because, number one, I do not believe that the Bible does pre-date a time in which material creation will be restored to some pristine situation. I believe the focus of all eschatology, as I have stated, I believe the focus of all eschatology has to do with man's covenant relationship, man's soteriological relationship with God.

Now, I really honestly don't know how much to address this issue. James says at some point the gospel would go on everywhere. Jesus obviously said that the gospel would be preached all over the world, then comes the end. I know that James believes that the gospel was preached in all the world in that generation, and then the end was in the first century.

Well, you see, what that means to me, what I read from that is that James must create a second great commission, after that one, after what Jesus said. His great commission to be fulfilled before the end of the fall of Jerusalem in AD70 before this eschaton. And now there's going to be another proclamation of the gospel into all the world then there's going to be another eschaton. Well I don't find that.

What I do find is that Jesus gave the promise that the gospel would be preached in all the world, the end would come and as a result of that, after the end of the age came and in the age to come the gospel would continue to be preached unendingly. Look at Revelation 21 and 22, where after the time of the end, after the end of the millennium in Revelation 20, after the New Jerusalem comes down from God, and for God to dwell with them, the gates of the city are always open.

Why are the gates of the city always open? So that the nations may come into the city. What do they come into the city for? Well, there happens to be a tree of life there beside a river of water, and that tree of life bears fruit twelve months a year.

By the way, that's the continuance of time isn't it? It bears fruit twelve months a year– time marches on. Time doesn't end – it is endless time. What is the fruit of that tree for? For the healing of the nations. Now remember, this is after the end. This is the nations being brought to Jesus Christ for a healing and redemption, continuing redemption after the end. This is not typological, this is ultimate, and there is continuing evangelism, continuing soteriology beyond the end.

All right. Well, James addresses the issue of the marriage which we have discussed a little bit, and he says, there was a marriage at Sinai. Well there was. I agree with that. Exodus 19 is absolutely beautiful in that regard. However, you see, God divorced Israel and then he said He would marry Israel again.

The great question is when did God place that marriage? Let me reiterate a point that I made yesterday with my chart, and that is that the promise of the marriage belonged to Israel. OK. It belonged to Israel. Hosea 2:19f, Isaiah 61, Isaiah 62, and there are other passages about this.

So when Jesus came promising the wedding, Jesus was not promising something that was new; he wasn't divorcing, if you'll let me use a pun, he wasn't divorcing the promise of the wedding from the promises that God had made to Israel. He was reiterating those promises made to Israel. And where does John place that wedding, that consummative wedding? Well in Revelation 19 we have the depiction of the destruction of Babylon, the city where the Lord was slain. Chapter 21 presents it all over again, recapitulates the issue, and John said, I saw the New Jerusalem coming down from God out of heaven adorned as a bride prepared for her husband. The time of the wedding is placed strictly within the context of the fall of Jerusalem *after the millennium.*

So this promise, the fulfillment of Israel's promise, and by the way, John reminds us in Revelation 22: 6, that he is stating his messages from the God of the prophets which is John's way of saying, look folks, I'm not saying anything new. I'm telling you what I've laid out here in this prophetic vision is what the prophets anticipated.

And what did he say about it? "Behold, I come quickly." That was the ending message and this promise of this judgment of all men and what does John envision, what is the message of Revelation 22:13f? "The Spirit and the bride say come."; "All things are ready."

The time of the wedding was present. It wasn't going to be postponed for a thousand years, two thousand years, or more. The time of the wedding was at hand. James says I don't think 2 Peter 3, I'm not going to get into this because he just brought it up, and I don't want to introduce a whole lot of material, but he did make a comment along the line and since he said it, I can respond to it. But he said, I really believe 2 Peter 3 is AD70, but that there's going to come a time when righteousness fully reigns.

Well Peter, I don't that Peter says we're looking for something in AD70 and something beyond that. He says, wherefore "according to his promise, we look for a new heaven and new earth wherein dwells righteousness." That's the world of righteousness promised by Isaiah 65.

My question is, what is the evidence for Peter saying, "Now AD70's going to be a type of what's really coming"? No, they were looking for the consummation of Israel's promises.
So, in the few remaining moments that I have, let me go back over the territory that I have covered, let me drive it home if I may

Let me suggest again to you that James has tried to deny it, but I would still suggest to you that James' eschatology does in fact posit Christian eschatology. Because he posits a radical disjunction, a radical transformation of the current Christian age in which the church as it now exists does not exist and function in the age to come.

And by the way, I return to the point that I made, the Bible only knows two ages, and we are in what they call the age to come. And it not only has no end, it will not be removed, that is, radically eschatologically transformed.

Israel was radically eschatologically transformed, Hebrews 12. But Hebrews tells us that the kingdom of Jesus Christ which they were then receiving would not be moved, i.e. in other words, look at what happened or what was about to happen to the Old Covenant world of Israel – radical eschatological transformation. It was "removed," it was shaken. But God said concerning the kingdom that they were then receiving that it would not be shaken, it would not be moved, which means it would not undergo and will not undergo radical eschatological transformation. Now all futurists paradigms say that the church will one day go to a radical eschatological transformation, but that is in direct violation of what Hebrews 12 says.

James says Israel's eschaton was in AD70. Well, I agree with that. But Israel's eschaton is the ultimate eschatological resurrection of 1 Corinthians 15. That's what Paul says.

I hope and I pray, literally, that we can finally catch the power of realizing that Paul said "my hope is nothing but what Moses and all of the prophets said would happen." We do an incredible disservice, it seems to me, to biblical eschatology and to biblical redemption if we seek to mitigate, if we seek to misplace, and if we seek to re-identify Biblical eschatology, and say OK Israel's eschaton was back there. OK. God stood with Israel, and to then say that the resurrection which was the hope of Israel is yet future.

Now, if you're like me, I was raised in a tradition, the churches of Christ tradition, in which we said openly, and my brethren in the church of Christ still say it, God was through with the Israel at the cross. Well, he might have been through with them at AD70, maybe in some sort of way, kind of, but point of fact is, God was through with Israel at AD70, but we're still looking for the resurrection.

Now I want to tell you something. I ask my brethren in the churches of Christ all of the time: Are all of God's promises to Old Covenant Israel fulfilled, and they tell me, oh absolutely, positively!; just as I asked James here.

My brethren answer, "Yes, all of God's promises have been fulfilled." Then I point out that the promise of the resurrection was a promise made to Israel. Well I can tell you, my brethren start stuttering and stammering and many of them say, "Well I think I hear my mamma calling me," and that's kind of the end of the conversation.

I'm being facetious, of course, trying to inject a little bit of levity. But you see, this really is a central issue. James' stated agreement that all of God's promises to Israel were fulfilled in AD70. But folks, the promise of the resurrection, the eschatological end-of-the-millennium resurrection was a promise made to Old Covenant Israel.

Furthermore, remember this: Jesus said not one single iota of the law, and that's the Old Covenant, Levitical, Mosaical, cultic world, the entirety of the Old Covenant world, not one iota of it could pass away until every single part of it, every bit of it was fulfilled.

Now the resurrection, the final, eschatological, end-of-the-millennium resurrection was a part of the law. How do I know that? Because Paul says so in Acts 24: "I believe all things that are written in the law and in the prophets, there's about to be the resurrection of the just and of the unjust."

Now since Jesus stated unequivocally that not so much as the tiniest particle of the Old Law could pass until every single part of the Old Law was fulfilled, and since the resurrection, the final eschatological end-of-the-millennium resurrection, belonged to the Old Covenant promises, was part and parcel of it, part of the warp and the woof of that Old Covenant world, then unless that resurrection, unless that end-of-the-millennium resurrection has occurred, then every single aspect of that Old Covenant world including the high priest's access, including the animal sacrifices, every single iota, every single particle of it stands valid today.

If we take the position as I do, as James does, that the entire Mosaic world was removed in AD70, I suggest to you that to be consistent we must agree and admit that the final eschatological coming of Jesus Christ and the attendant resurrection from the dead occurred at the time of the fall of Jerusalem in AD70.

Thank you very much.

www.ingramcontent.com/pod-product-compliance
Lightning Source LLC
Chambersburg PA
CBHW060303050426
42448CB00009B/1740